ALSO BY JOHN GIERACH

DUMB LUCK AND THE KINDNESS OF STRANGERS

JOHN GIERACH

Art by Glenn Wolff

Simon & Schuster
New York   London   Toronto   Sydney   New Delhi

Simon & Schuster
1230 Avenue of the Americas
New York, NY 10020

First Simon & Schuster hardcover edition April 2020

SIMON & SCHUSTER and colophon are registered trademarks
of Simon & Schuster, Inc.

For information about special discounts for bulk purchases,
please contact Simon & Schuster Special Sales at 1-866-506-1949
or business@simonandschuster.com.

The Simon & Schuster Speakers Bureau can bring authors to your
live event. For more information or to book an event, contact the
Simon & Schuster Speakers Bureau at 1-866-248-3049
or visit our website at www.simonspeakers.com.

Manufactured in the United States of America

10 9 8 7 6 5 4 3 2 1

Library of Congress Cataloging-in-Publication Data is available.

ISBN 978-1-5011-6858-1
ISBN 978-1-5011-6859-8 (ebook)

I no longer require a wished-for future
to cancel the present.
—DONALD HALL

CONTENTS

DUMB LUCK AND THE KINDNESS OF STRANGERS

1.

CLOSE TO HOME

I live in the foothills of the northern Colorado Rockies with dozens of trout streams within day-trip range, so it's easy for me to recommend fishing close to home. The advantages are obvious. You can play hooky to go fishing at a moment's notice; it only takes one trip to the pickup to pack your minimal gear (you know how little you need because you need so little); you know right where you want to go and have plenty of backups in case someone has high-graded your spot; and a rained-out day isn't a deal breaker—you just go home and come back when the creek clears. Eventually fishing becomes such a normal part of daily life that you can stop for a half gallon of milk on the way home.

I understand that not everyone is so lucky; a precious few have it easier, but most have it harder. I might once have said that you make that kind of luck for yourself, and in some ways you do, but it's just as often true that people end up where they are through no fault of their own and are then faced with making the best of it.

I know that because I've temporarily ended up in a few places I didn't care for over the years (Cleveland comes immediately to mind), but I was young and unattached enough to be able to move on as soon as I comprehended my predicament. I may also have understood that the option to move on would begin to wane with the accumulation of possessions and entanglements, which at the time only made the idea of blowing town seem more attractive. In fact, there were a number of years when literally or figuratively blowing town at the slightest provocation was my modus operandi.

I didn't exactly weigh all my options before I finally bought property and sank roots where I am now; it was just that when the opportunity came for that to happen I liked where I was and thought, *Why not?* I'd recently turned thirty and my father had died, leaving me a small inheritance: two things I didn't see coming. A few years earlier this might have gone differently, but by then I was just old enough to realize I only had two choices here: wake up in five years dead broke and with an epic hangover, or spend the whole wad on something I could hold on to and make use of, like a house. There were those in my family who said my modest windfall would be enough for a down payment on a nice little starter home in a decent neighborhood, but they'd overlooked my position as someone with no credit rating who'd be hard-pressed to convince a bank that I was "employed" as a freelance writer. Even I could see I wasn't the type to come up with a mortgage payment once a month like clockwork.

So I found a wretched but habitable little house with an asking price of about what I had on hand and bought it outright. It was the cheapest house for sale in the county and with good reason, but it was within walking distance of a sleepy little town I liked and across the road from a trout stream I fished often, which made up for a lot. There was a tense moment when the seller balked—even though people weren't exactly lining up to buy this place—but in a rare burst of insight I realized he'd taken one look at me and assumed a cash transaction of this size must involve drug money. So I took him aside and straightened him out. He said he was sorry to hear about my dad and the deal went through.

As I said, I already knew and liked the stream across the road from my new house, but with a home base just downstream of the confluence of its three forks, I set out to explore the entire drainage as time permitted. The majority of it was on federal land—national forest, national park, and wilderness area—that was sometimes difficult to reach, but at least it was public. A few stretches lower down were private and had to be finessed in one way or another. (By that I mean I always at least tried to get permission.) The project went on for decades in a haphazard way and I can't swear that it was ever actually completed, but to this day if someone asks me what's down in here or way up there I can tell them in convincing detail.

Naturally I discovered some sweet spots that held good-size trout and where I never saw another soul and I believed—or wanted to believe—that these places were unknown to anyone except one young, intrepid trout bum. That was the kind of glamorous notion that's irresistible at a certain age, even though it stretches the bounds of belief.

Some years later, on a junket to Canada's Northwest Territories, a friend and I talked a guide into taking us to some bona fide virgin water. It was a feeder creek that the lodge we were fishing from—the only lodge that had ever operated in the region—knew for sure they'd never taken sports to. Furthermore, this wasn't the kind of place First Nation netters would ever have gone; they'd have stuck with the bigger water that would be easier to fish and yield better hauls.

So we alternately paddled and walked a canoe a few miles up that creek, where we caught arctic grayling weighing around a pound each and some hammer-handle-size pike. The only thing that was exceptional about the place was that we were pretty sure we were the first ones to ever fish there. It was an ambition satisfied, but by then new ideas about preservation had stolen the romance from the notion of breaking new sod like a pioneer and replaced it with the sneaking suspicion that maybe we humans, with our monstrous egos and appetites, should leave a few places unspoiled. So I came away with mosquito bites and mixed feelings. I never felt guilty about fishing there, but I wasn't as pleased with myself as I'd expected to be and I dropped the part of the fantasy where I named the creek and then went on to live long enough to see that name on a map.

As time went on I worked hard, or at least steadily, traveled more, and finally reached a point where I actually *could* convince a bank I was gainfully employed as a writer. But I'd never developed the habit of borrowing, so the only time I actually did it I got so creeped out that I paid off the loan early, incidentally saving myself a pile in interest. As Craig Nova said, "Credit is a good friend, but a hard master, while cash is a constant like the speed of light."

Another constant was the water near home that I'd become thoughtlessly familiar with and felt I knew better than anyone. My evidence was—and still is—that when the streams are fishable I know where to go, what fly to tie on, and where and how to cast in order to catch trout. (More and bigger trout than any other competent fly-fisher could manage? I like to think so, but who's to say?)

Sometimes I'm even able to pick the species I feel like catching: brown trout lower down, shading to brook trout at higher elevations, and finally to some cutthroats holding on way up in the high country, where the streams are cold and narrow and the season is short. The transitions between species are indistinct; they occur at different elevations depending on the creek, and they'll sometimes move around from year to year, but seldom by more than a mile or so. Of course that's not counting fish that pop up unexpectedly where I've come to think they shouldn't be, but then however intimately you think you know a stream it can still surprise you.

A good-size trout in any of these creeks will be around 10 inches long, with plenty smaller and a few larger. A 12- or 14-incher is a real nice fish and in the forty-plus years I've fished here I've landed a handful in the neighborhood of 16 inches, including one lovely cutthroat that almost brought me to tears and probably would have if there hadn't been a witness present. And more recently there was an 18-inch brown that made me *glad* I had a witness along to measure the fish and back up my story. But even then we got looks from friends that suggested they thought we'd shared a recently legalized doobie and gotten hysterical about a 14-incher. I was insulted at first, but then decided that if anyone chose not to believe in the hidden pool where the big trout lives, it was okay with me.

I've caught larger and more exotic fish elsewhere. I wouldn't trade a minute of that, and plan to do it again as often as possible, but this modest, hometown water where the benchmark trout will always be around nine or 10 inches long is a fine thing to come home to, regardless of where I've been. This isn't the kind of destination water that attracts hordes of technicians and headhunters. It's fished mostly by locals and the odd tourist with a day to kill. For decades its well-deserved reputation for mediocrity has saved it, although that's not to say it hasn't changed.

In the years I've fished here there have been high runoffs, and one massive thousand-year flood that profoundly rearranged the drainage in places, not to mention droughts—some lasting as long as five seasons—plus all the other natural and man-made slings and arrows trout streams are heir to. In some big snowpack years the water stayed so high and cold that there was virtually no fishing season at all unless you wanted to resort to worms and sinkers. But fish eat well in high water, so the following year, after a more or less normal runoff receded, the trout were big and fat and there were lots of them. On the other hand, late in some drought years there was hardly enough water to keep a trout wet and by the following spring we'd lost whole age classes of larger fish to winterkill.

These are undammed streams, so it's all about rain and snow, heat and cold, absent the human greed, shortsightedness, and lawsuits that begin to kick in at the first irrigation head gates. Once the runoff comes down in a normal year, the online readout from the gauging stations forms a gentle wave: up slightly at night as the day's snowmelt reaches the gauge and down slightly during the day to reflect the cold, high-elevation nights. It looks like the slow heartbeat of a large animal at rest, disturbed only by the occasional thunderstorm.

Over time I've learned to hope for normal seasons, but enjoy the fat years all the more knowing they won't last and endure the poor ones in the equally secure knowledge that things will eventually turn around. I'm not sure this has taught me to take a longer philosophical view of things, but it's at least shown me the qualities of character that would require.

I no longer fish the stretch of the main branch that flows through town and past the place where my old house used to stand. Over the last thirty years there have been two so-called improvement projects done there. They were both undertaken by people with the best intentions and have attracted the attention of more fly-fishers, but what was once a pretty stretch of trout stream now looks like a suburban water feature and the fishing is nowhere near as good as it was under the regime of benign neglect this little river used to enjoy.

The once-sleepy little town has gone in the same direction. After the influx of peripheral hippies that I was part of came the yuppies, Gen Xers, millennials, and more recently hipsters with their big beards, flannel shirts, and skinny jeans; many of them are the kind that move to a town with dirt streets because they think it's charming, and then complain about the dust. Where there were once no stoplights, there are now four; where what passed for traffic once consisted of pickup trucks and big American sedans, there are now sometimes more bikes than cars, and the cup of coffee that used to cost a quarter now runs three dollars, although, to be fair, that's mostly just inflation and the coffee is a lot better than the dishwater-strength Folger's we used to get.

And speaking of inflation, the town can't grow much because it's surrounded on three sides by open public land, so real estate prices have climbed to meet the growing demands of gentrification, surprising the hell out of the few remaining natives. When the time finally came for me to cash out and blow town again, my old place was worth so much more than I'd paid for it—not the house (they bulldozed that within a week of the closing) but the land it sat on—that I could relocate north into the next county to a better old house on some acreage with more mule deer and rabbits than neighbors. A man in the business once told me that your best allies in real estate are longevity and the dumb luck to want out when others want in, and in fact this was the perfect move. I didn't even lose any of my home water. I just added twenty minutes to the commute.

I did briefly consider moving away entirely—maybe to one of the places where I'd fished for a week, caught bigger trout, and come back thinking, *You know, I could live there*—but it turns out I guessed right back in my thirties: the roots eventually grow too deep to be pulled up without permanent damage. So instead I became one of those guys who give directions like "Go through town and turn right where the old lumber yard used to be."

I now mostly stick to the upper forks of the drainage, through the canyons and on up into the headwaters, even though at least in their more accessible stretches some of these creeks have gotten noticeably more crowded. That's because the population of the state has more than doubled since I moved here and fly-fishing, which was still a sporting backwater in the 1970s, is now as fashionable as skiing. So people keep moving here because it's a beautiful place to live, but no one ever leaves for the same reason. The upshot is that it's ever so slightly less beautiful than it once was, although you wouldn't notice that if you hadn't been here all along to see it happen.

And yes, it's disheartening to find a stranger standing in what was once your secret pool and it's either more or less disheartening in direct relation to how much trouble you went through to get there. Consequently, it's easy to conclude that this upstart is fishing it all wrong, although it's best not to hang around and watch, hoping to have that opinion verified. We local fishermen are widely believed (if not by others, then at least by ourselves) to have our home waters wired, but as Robert Traver pointed out, sometimes it's the out-of-town nimrods who come in with fresh eyes, new ideas, and the latest fly patterns and proceed to fish circles around us. That does sting a little, but the deeper wound is that what were once our little secrets have become common knowledge.

For a long time the obvious solution to more people was simply to go earlier and hike farther than anyone else, thereby outdistancing the competition. That still works, but it now takes longer. I noticed that at some point the strategy of hiking farther and the reality of getting older began to diverge in inconvenient ways. It sneaks up on you, but eventually a mile at altitude begins to feel like a mile and a half, then two miles, and so on. I won't dwell on this, but if you're still curious you should read the late Donald Hall's excellent book *Essays after Eighty*. It will either ease your fears about old age or make you vow to shoot yourself at age seventy-nine.

I suspect that I now fish this water differently than I did more than four decades ago, although I'm not sure I can put a finger on exactly how. It's true that we all develop a fishing style tailored to the water we're most familiar with—ranging from balls-to-the-wall to methodical to meditative—but it's also true that every day out constitutes its own little self-contained drama and no two are exactly alike.

Some days I fish with a kind of quasi-scientific curiosity, casting to every inch of water and noting where the takes come from as if I were studying the characteristics of holding water. Other days I move right along, cherry-picking the known honey holes, calling my shots, congratulating myself when I'm right, and instantly forgetting about it when I'm wrong. Usually I'll fish a size 14 or 16 dry fly trailing a lightly weighted soft hackle dropper of the same size. Other days I'll just fish the dry fly, wanting to hook only those trout that are willing to come the full distance to the surface, if only because the take is such a pretty sight.

When I'm fishing with certain friends we'll leapfrog from pool to pool and compare notes later. With others we're more likely to trade off, with one of us casting and the other offering commentary like an announcer at a chess tournament, only not as serious.

When I'm fishing alone I'll occasionally just walk the creek waiting for some sign to start casting and figuring I'll know it when I see it. Sometimes it's as obvious as a sputtering hatch and a pod of rising trout. Other times it's something peripheral, like a patch of ripe raspberries or a few doorknob-size boletus mushrooms so small and fresh they're not yet wormy, that makes me stop. (I carry brown paper bags in my daypack for these finds, although often enough I'll just graze on the berries on-site.) On rare days it's something as vague as a quality of the light or a certain stillness in the air that seems to make the water vibrate with possibility, but I think that's less mystical than it sounds. It's just that some of the things you know about your home water operate beneath the level of full consciousness and only reveal themselves disguised as intuition.

Sometimes I even have dreams about these creeks. In one that woke me up bolt upright before dawn I hook a fish so big that when I tighten the line and the fish begins to struggle I realize the bed of the stream I'm standing on is actually the fish's back. I look down to see that the fist-size cobbles have turned to black spots on a bronze background, which would make this a brown trout the size of a school bus. That's it; there's no plot, no story line, just that one image that leaves me awake and blinking. Sometimes I have dreams so inexplicable that I assume they were meant for someone else and leaked into my head by accident, but that one—whatever it means— is mine alone.

I do love to catch trout—it becomes a hard habit to break—but more often now I find myself going out close to home not to clean up on fish, but just to prove to myself that they're still there. So far they always have been, although they're more or less cooperative depending on a hundred variables that can change by the hour. But in fact, these creeks near home have held up better over more than half my lifetime than anything else I can think of.

I no longer wonder, as I once did, how things might have gone if I'd settled somewhere else: maybe on a bigger, snazzier watershed that people travel long distances to reach hoping for blanket hatches and trout that regularly crack 20 inches. I can and do go to places like that when I get the chance and when I get back home I'm happy where I am.

I only have one friend that I've known for as long as I've fished my home water. We don't see that much of each other anymore, but when we do get together—usually to go fishing—we pick right up in the middle of a nearly half-century-long conversation that will end only with one of our funerals. I've fished a lot of places and met a lot of people, but there are only a handful of streams that I know inside out and an equally small number of people whom I consider to be close friends. But a few of each is enough when you're loyal as a dog to all of them.

2.

SHOULDER SEASON

A low pressure front from the Pacific Northwest had hung up on the nearby Continental Divide like a kite in a tree and pieces of it were tearing off and blowing east over the river. For a while there'd be bright but ineffective sunlight from a chilly blue sky and the river would seem dead; then a bank of slate-colored clouds and spitting snow would sail in on a colder breeze, shading the river, dropping the temperature, and triggering a flurry of Blue-wing Olive mayflies and rising trout.

While it was cloudy I'd cast my brace of small dry flies, mending my line to get a down-and-across-stream drift against the far bank where some feeding trout were stacked up. When the sun came back out and the rise sputtered to a stop, I'd furl my leader and stand waiting for the next squall with my mind at first racing impatiently, then gradually slowing, and finally idling like a car waiting at a stoplight. The sunlight felt warm in an indecisive way and the air smelled piney, but with a metallic edge from the lingering chill. It would have been a beautiful early spring day in the Rockies except that the fish had stopped biting.

That was last year on a river I fish often in the spring because it's only twenty miles from home, so I can drop everything to run up there when the weather turns snarky enough to bring on a hatch. I remember that specific day because the cloud cover was like an on/off switch and it was a vivid example of how weather-dependent these little mayflies are. It was the kind of episode you'd invent to illustrate the point if you were the kind of storyteller who invented things.

This was in mid-April, when the first migrating hummingbirds begin to arrive from Central America, the first bears awake from hibernation looking skinny and befuddled, income taxes come due, and the Blue-wing Olive hatches begin to dribble off on days when the weather suits them. I don't recall how many trout I caught that day, but I'll guess that, as usual, I hooked and landed a fraction of the strikes I got, so it wouldn't have been many. The browns and rainbows in this hard-fished catch-and-release tailwater have learned the neat trick of being in two places at once like certain subatomic particles, allowing them to eat your fly but be somewhere else entirely when you set the hook.

Getting out in this shoulder season is one of the great low-key pleasures of the sport. Conditions are often so far from perfect that you can't reasonably expect more than a pleasantly fishless walk along a river where, without fretting too much about success, you can work out the off-season kinks in your casting, get your river legs back, and relocate the leaks in your waders you forgot to patch last fall. If you happen to guess the weather and the seasonal timing right and a little hatch sputters off, good; you made the right call. Even better if you hang a trout or two and better yet if there's no one else on the river so that on what might have been just another day, you can drive home feeling cagey. Sure, the fishing could have been better, but when you're out early like this a few small trout against the odds seem more in the spirit of the season than lots of bigger ones. That will come soon enough, but for now it's best to ease in slowly. It's barely spring here at an elevation of 7,500 feet, with remnant snow still lingering in the shade, and November, when it all begins to wind down again, seems like a lifetime away.

Here in Colorado it's entirely up to you when you decide to get out, since there's no closed fishing season like there was in the Midwest, where I grew up. Back there it was all about opening day, which some in my family took seriously and others considered— along with bag limits and no trespassing signs—to be no more than suggestions. When I bought my first resident fishing license here in 1969, I asked the man behind the counter when the season opened. He said, "It never closes. You can fish any day of the year you can stand to be out there." I'd never heard of such a thing, but it seemed like a crucial element of the hippie utopia we envisioned back then: no Big Brother telling you when you could or couldn't go fishing.

I was pretty footloose in those days and hadn't so much moved to Colorado as just sort of washed up here, but I remember putting the license in my wallet, walking out into a cold late winter afternoon, and thinking—in a voice that sounded suspiciously like that of a favorite uncle—*Boy, I believe you've landed in the right place.*

Not long after that I became what they used to call a "frostbite fisherman": someone who fishes with a fly rod from November through February just because rivers below bottom-draw dams stay open and marginally fishable through the winter. This was usually a matter of dredging small nymphs with split shot on the leader while your line froze in the guides and your feet went numb in your waders, although if you spent enough time on the water a rise of trout to a midge hatch wasn't out of the question. It seemed worth doing because it was not only possible to catch trout on flies in the winter, but it was legal.

I haven't entirely given that up, but I now think more in terms of the early Olive and midge hatches that hold out more hope of fishing a floating fly. I've never been quite the dry fly purist I once pretended to be—there are too many other interesting ways to catch fish on a fly rod—but nymphing comes in fourth for me after stripping streamers, swinging wet flies, and of course drifting a dry fly. I don't really think dry flies are superior to other fishing techniques, but I *do* think that tying on a floating fly and waiting for a hatch reintroduces an element of restraint that's been missing from the sport over the last few decades.

This is a stance that seems more common among older fishermen. I recently got a handwritten letter from an artist I know who said he hadn't emailed because he "doesn't do screens"—this less than a year after the last poet I knew who still wrote on a typewriter died in his eighties. More to the point, a writer whom I've read for years but only recently met on the Bitterroot River in April said he "Doesn't do nymphs." I said, "Me neither," which wasn't strictly true, but close enough. So we fished floating Skwala stonefly patterns on a cold day when nymphs would surely have gotten us into more than the one brown trout we landed that day, but neither of us was sorry. They say getting older is a process of elimination and I wonder if we eventually start defining ourselves solely in terms of what we won't do.

It was a month earlier, in March, when my artist friend Bob White and I went to the Green River in Utah. Bob lives in Minnesota, and although he knew the Green by reputation, he'd never fished it. I *had* fished it a few times years ago, but it was always six weeks later when the Blue-wing Olive hatch was in full swing and the seasonal crowds of fishermen caused trailer jams at the boat ramps and traffic problems on the water.

Back then we fished with a fine guide named Denny Breer, a large, broad-shouldered, good-natured man who was more philosophical than I was about this. We'd get out early before the worst of the rush, and when the crowd caught up with us Denny would simply beach his wooden drift boat and we'd drink coffee and talk while they pounded on through. Ten minutes after the last boat went around the bend, the trout that had been put down would begin to rise tentatively. Ten minutes after that they'd be back in their feeding rhythm and Denny would say, "Okay, you guys ready?"

This was a strategy designed to win the battle by not fighting it, as well as an object lesson in the idea that other fishermen aren't necessarily your adversary, except maybe in the sense that humanity in general is its own worst enemy.

Those were good days of fishing. The long hatches were thick enough to get the trout feeding eagerly, but not so thick that they wouldn't notice your fly, and the fish were good-size and strong. Still, months later I'd catch myself recalling the traffic in more detail than the fishing, so after a couple of spring trips I stopped going back.

But then Bob and I got an invitation from a man named Spencer out there in Dutch John, Utah. The word was that the Olives might already be starting to come off by then, and if not we could always fish streamers. Furthermore, it would be early enough that almost no one would be on the water except for a few locals sneaking out ahead of the onslaught of tourists.

It was all true. At the huge paved ramp below the dam there was only one other boat, a raft crewed by a man, a woman, and a young Australian shepherd wearing a doggie life jacket with a suitcase handle on the back. I tried saying hello to the dog, but he was too busy overseeing preparations for the float to be bothered with an out-of-towner. The same could be said of the people. Some locals in the West have a way of observing "You ain't from around here" that's not exactly unfriendly, but still freighted with meaning.

Our days started slowly, as days do in March. First we'd linger over big breakfasts at the café in town, then we'd dawdle near the put-in, slowly swinging streamers in the quieter water and drawing the occasional halfhearted nip from one of the smaller fish. It would only be later in the morning when the cold water warmed a few crucial degrees that the larger trout would begin to get curious, if not actually aggressive.

The action would pick up gradually as the morning wore on. We fished light-colored weighted streamers on sink-tip lines, casting them against the steep banks and letting them sink several feet before starting a retrieve. The days were cold and overcast with no glare on the surface and nearly unlimited visibility in the clear water, so we could see everything. Through trial and error we settled on a slow, uneven retrieve as the best tactic. On the first few inquisitive follows I got I sped up my strip hoping to trigger a predatory response, but although a few trout tumbled for that old trick, most turned away as if chasing the fly in that cold water was more trouble than it was worth.

The trout we got to the net were good-size and solid, mostly browns, but also a few big-shouldered rainbows. These fish didn't fight all that hard, but you get used to that. Back in the frostbite days some fishermen wondered if they were unduly stressing trout by catching them from freezing cold water. But when I asked a fisheries biologist about that, he said it was the opposite, that catching fish in *warm* water stressed them. "If they seem sluggish when it's cold," he said, "it just means you can land 'em quicker and release 'em sooner." He added that although he'd never seen any studies, he'd be willing to bet that the rate of accidental hooking mortality goes up in the summer and down in the winter.

The canyon we were floating through is famously scenic and Spencer said Bob must be getting great material for his paintings. I said no doubt, but probably not the kind of thing that would be endorsed by the Chamber of Commerce. John Wesley Powell named this stretch the Flaming Gorge for the way the tall red-rock canyon walls lit up in the morning sun, but after looking at hundreds of Bob's paintings and hanging several of them on my walls at home, I thought he'd pass up the traditionally spectacular scenery in favor of something more along the lines of maroon-barked dogwoods and leafless gray willows under uncertain late winter light.

Sometime in midafternoon when the days had warmed as much as they were going to, a few small Olive mayflies would begin to pop off and we'd start scanning eddies and the tail-outs of riffles for rising trout. There were never many—just scattered small pods of fish here and there leaving quiet rings on the surface—but it was all we needed to switch to the dry fly rods that we'd carried all day in the rod racks. As efficient as the streamers and sinking lines had been, it would take me only a few false casts to remember how much a fly rod loves a dry fly.

We never got many trout this way—there weren't a lot of risers to begin with and they were easy to put down with a bad drift or a missed strike—but we'd invariably land some nice ones; heavy fish that fought well, and then hung sluggishly in the net to let themselves be released. And then, after an hour or two, the wind would pick up, the temperature would drop, there'd be a leaden change in the light as the sun began to drop invisibly behind the thick lid of clouds and it would be over. We'd drift along scanning the water for a while longer, but the bugs and the rising trout would be gone. Eventually our predatory attentiveness would soften into sightseeing and we'd float the last mile or so to the takeout with a wider view of things, idly thinking about how it would feel to settle into the cab of the pickup with the heater going.

On our last night Bob and I slept in our room in Dutch John to the sound of sleet on the roof and in the morning it was raining with fresh snow visible on the slopes above us. Spencer decided to drive us back to the airport in Salt Lake City by a longer route that would avoid the icy passes by looping through a corner of southwestern Wyoming. This was rolling marginal pastureland punctuated here and there by fence rows, shelter belts, and tree lines marking water-courses, the distances magnified and the colors muted by a curtain of drizzle. There were few cars on the county road and no visible activity at the scattered small spreads we passed, but on a day when the bustle of ranch life had been temporarily brought indoors, lights burned in kitchen windows and outbuildings. We were two hours into the drive and had talked ourselves out when, after we'd ridden along in silence for quite a while, Bob muttered, "Everywhere I look I see Russell Chatham landscapes."

A few weeks later I was in Missoula, Montana, at a Trout Un-limited event, after which two guys from the club named Mark and Mike took me fishing. (I'm normally bad with names, but "M&M" immediately came to mind as a workable mnemonic.) These trout clubs like to hold their events before the season's fishing gets started so their members will still be in town, meaning the fishing possi-bilities were slim, but these guys had settled on a twenty-mile float down the Flathead River on the reservation that sounded inter-esting. Mark said that hardly anyone fished there this early in the season, that there was a small population of brown trout—as few as ten fish per mile by one account—but that for reasons he didn't fully understand, they were all big. I liked the sound of it. I've always had a gambler's weak spot for a shot at a big payoff on long odds.

It was a cold day with a stiff, bitter breeze. Within a mile of the put-in we were bundled in every piece of spare clothing we'd brought and happy for the exertion of rowing or lobbing 8-weight rods to help keep us warm. This stretch of river flowed placidly through open, rolling prairie with a riparian fringe of pine, juniper, and cottonwood that made it seem hidden from the big world. I was told that in the summer there's some recreational boat traffic ("recreational" meaning there's plenty of beer on board) but on this cold day we had it to ourselves and it was easy to imagine that no one ever came here.

We cast streamers along the banks and stripped them back toward the boat. The casting was so repetitive and the strikes and follows were so few and far between that the fishing became automatic and I now and then had to remind myself to put a little life in my retrieves. This didn't have the look of rich water and we wondered what these trout were eating, finally deciding that all rivers have their secrets: schools of baitfish, vast herds of crawdads, or some such thing. Whatever it was, there must have been a lot of them because the trout were built like footballs with small heads on round, hard bodies. As predicted, there weren't many of them, but they were all big. Our smallest was around 19 inches, the largest 23, and all heavy for their size—each one well worth the effort and the long wait between strikes.

Lunch was a high point: a wonderfully spicy stew Mark had made with moose shank, heated up on a camp stove in the partial shelter of a copse of junipers, backed up by cheese, hard salami, and black coffee. Later, back on the river, we spotted a short-eared owl on its perch in a cottonwood, sizing us up uncharitably with his yellow eyes—three men in a boat passing at current speed: no more than a momentary annoyance.

At the takeout a passing tribal ranger parked his big Dodge pickup on the dirt road and ambled over to strike up a conversation. While we broke down our gear and trailered the boat he talked about the vast amount of country he was expected to patrol on his own, his family, the people he knew, the wildlife he'd seen, and some of the odd folks he'd run into out there, as well as the inexplicable shenanigans he'd busted some of them for. This was dragging on, but it was a good story, by turns scary, poignant, and hilarious, and I wondered if we were listening to a book proposal.

After half an hour he finally checked our licenses and tribal permits almost as an afterthought. Then he seemed to notice it was getting dark and we were all packed up, so by way of letting us go he said, "Well, I was glad to run into you guys. This time of year I got no one to talk to."

3.

THE LEASE

Some friends and I lease a half mile of mountain trout stream that winds across a willow-choked basin at an elevation of 8,500 feet. It's not quite flat enough through there to be called a meadow stretch, but it's flatter, wider, and more meandering than the steep water in the canyons above and below, and the wide-open view of the Continental Divide to the west is as corny as a stage set. The property is owned by a rustically fancy lodge that's been in business continuously for more than a hundred years, although, as is often the case with these old log buildings, the current lodge is built on the ashes of the old one that burned down. This place has been through several incarnations in that time, but it's now an "events center" that makes its nut in the summer by hosting outdoor weddings with a 14,000-foot mountain as a backdrop.

The stream was leased for a few years by a local outfitter who guided there. In its natural state this water produces feral brown and brook trout not much longer than about nine or 10 inches, but every spring this guy would dump in some big, fat hatchery rainbows for the clients. To his credit, he never actually claimed that these were "wild Rocky Mountain trout," but he'd fess up only if he was asked, leaving the uninquisitive free to believe whatever made them happy.

Then one year the outfitter dropped the lease and my friend Doug took it over for a token fee that was about what it was worth as a trout stream, but far less than they probably could have gotten for it. That's because the woman who now owns the lodge doesn't care about the fishing one way or the other and would probably just let people fish through if it weren't for the weddings. These are momentous occasions that are fraught with nerves and emotion by nature and the picture-book setting has plenty of built-in drama of its own. At that elevation howling wind can come up suddenly—playing hell with hairdos and flower arrangements—and mountain storms complete with rain, hail, and lightning can pounce in the time it takes to ask, "Was that thunder?" For that matter, it wouldn't be impossible for an oblivious moose or curious bear to crash the ceremony, although I've never heard of that happening. Given those risks, the last thing you want is for the proceedings to be marred by something preventable, like a fisherman yelling "Fuck!" when he misses a strike or being discovered by the mother of the bride as he pees in the bushes.

So our agreement is that we get the place cheap in return for keeping it posted. (There was a time when this could have been done with a handshake, but those folks whose word could be taken to the bank are dying off, so now everyone seems more comfortable when money changes hands.) Beyond that, we can fish it whenever we want to as long as we never allow ourselves to be seen or heard by a member of a wedding party. It goes without saying that the short high country fishing and wedding seasons coincide almost exactly.

From the bridge at the downstream end of the property there's about an hour's worth of careful pocket-water fishing up to the Rock Pool, which is the premier honey hole. There are some obvious feeding lies in here that almost always hold fish and there's the usual temptation to cherry-pick, but we've learned to prospect and on a good day a trout or two will come out of spots where we don't remember ever catching one before. There are a few places where the wading gets gnarly and you'd like to loop around on the bank, but the willows here are as thick and impenetrable as the wedding venue is manicured and we've let whatever rough trails there were grow over.

The Rock Pool itself is a big, open, fishy run that two people can cast to at once, but where we usually trade off strike for strike to make it last. The sweet spot here isn't in the dark run against the big granite boulder, where you'd expect it to be, but a few yards up from the tail-out where the bottom shallows up and the current begins to accelerate. If you were with an out-of-town guest who didn't know the score you could hook the biggest trout yourself while still appearing to generously give up the best water. If you were that kind of friend, that is.

Above that is some riffly water with scattered shallow pockets that sometimes hold small trout and about midway up this stretch is where you come in sight of the footbridge that leads from the lodge building to the clearing on the south side of the stream where the weddings are held. This is where you stop to watch and listen. Usually it's well-dressed people crossing the bridge that gives it away.

(Guests and members of the wedding stroll like royalty; caterers and other functionaries scurry.) But it could also be voices, laughter, music, tinkling champagne glasses, and so on. Not to sound like a steely-eyed mountain man or anything, but no one who knows the difference between the natural sights and sounds of the mountains and an episode of *Downton Abbey* could stumble into the middle of things from here without knowing it.

Of course the easiest thing would be to take an extra five minutes to drive past the lodge before we start fishing to see if the parking lot is full, indicating a wedding in progress, but we hardly ever do that. Maybe we just enjoy spying and then slinking away through the underbrush like desperados.

If the stream is fishing well that day we'll walk back downstream to the pickup, drive around to the bridge at the top end of the property, and get back in there. If it's *not* fishing well, we'll go somewhere else nearby or, if it's late or a storm has blown up, just go home, but we usually drive to the top end anyway to see if the no trespassing signs there need replacing.

They don't last forever. After too long in high-altitude summer sunlight and winter wind a sign will fade like an old photo and begin to look halfhearted, as if someone might have cared about trespassing once, but maybe not so much anymore. And sometimes people tear them down, either on general principles or so that if they're caught fishing where they shouldn't, they can say, "Well, there was no sign . . ."

I was never one to tear down signs, but I did trespass here a few times way back before the outfitter and the wedding business at the lodge. I used to fish the public water upstream in the national forest, and sometimes when I'd come back down at the end of the day I'd see trout rising in the bend pool that's visible from the bridge. I understood in a vague way that this was private property—or at least that the road was the eastern forest boundary—but a narrow trail led down to the water and in those days there was no fence and it wasn't posted. If I'd ever been yelled at, that's what I'd have said: "Well, there was no sign . . ." I guess it's ironic that I had a hand in putting up the no trespassing signs that are there now, but then life is funny that way.

That bend pool you see from the bridge can be good, especially late in the day when there are some caddis or mayflies around. Sometimes trout will lie in the riffly current on the inside of the bend, and there's a slot of deep holding water against the outside bank that can be good for a bigger fish. It's easy to hook a fly in the bushes here, and then stand there wondering whether to break it off and lose the fly or wade over to get it and blow the pool. At the bottom of this run there's a log jam with a deep, eddying backwater that's always good for a fish if you can get the tricky cast and drift right with deep wading, high sticking, and a favorable breeze. There's some interesting braided pocket water below that, but before long you come within sight of the footbridge again with its strollers and scurriers and that's where any gate crasher with an ounce of sense will turn around.

There are also several good-looking pools right behind the lodge, but the wedding business has been booming lately, so we don't get to fish there very often. The good news is that by the time we do get to them—usually in September—the pools have been rested for months, so the innocence of the fish offsets the spooky, low water conditions. The bad news is, I think that in recent years some of the lodge employees have taken to fishing bait there after work, so by late summer there aren't many trout left.

The first year we had this lease a few of those big rainbows the outfitter had stocked were still holding on against the odds. Every once in a while you'd see one sulking on the bottom of a pool, apparently deep in some kind of private funk. They were stubbornly uncatchable, as if they'd given up on the effort of either feeding or spooking. Maybe they understood as well as we did that if there was enough food and winter holding water here to support big trout, there'd have already *been* big trout, and so they were doomed. By the second summer they were all gone and I was glad not to see them anymore. They made me sad.

What was left were the browns and brook trout whose ances-tors had been planted back in the dark days of western fish culture when it was thought that one trout was as good as another and so the indigenous cutthroats all but vanished. Browns were native to Eu-rope and brook trout to northeastern North America, but these fish have lived wild in the West for so long that calling them nonnative now seems like a technical distinction. Brook trout especially were stocked here from the beginning—off the books as often as not—and they're still the most common trout in the small, high-altitude streams of the Rockies. In many places they're what we've had for more than a century. They're probably the fish that were already here when they built the original lodge around the turn of the last century, dumped in as fingerlings after all the cutthroats had gone into the frying pan.

There are five of us in the lease, but the only two I ever see are Doug and Vince. Doug runs a small corporation and he's one of the hardest-working people I know because he doesn't delegate well. (I once asked him what his role at the company was and he said, "I'm the only adult in the room.") Consequently, his fishing time is lim-ited and he likes the lease because he can go up there on a Saturday or Sunday when the public water can get crowded and have it to himself. Public water does sometimes get crowded around here on summer weekends and it's handy to have a spot in your back pocket where you won't see anyone else—or if you do, you can tell them to leave.

Vince is retired from a middle management job, but he's busier now than when he was employed. His projects include, but aren't limited to, building an addition to his log house, refinishing an old wooden drift boat, making split bamboo fly rods, and managing an irrigation ditch—a job that, even in the twenty-first century, still carries the title of "ditch rider": all jobs that are custom made for a hard-working perfectionist. When I say I "had a hand" in putting up those no trespassing signs, I mean Vince did the work so it would be done right, while I stood there offering encouragement and handing him the tools he asked for. That pretty much describes every job we've ever done together.

Vince always used to fish the lease with his great old dog Gabe. Gabe was the dog of a lifetime: quiet, patient, loyal, self-sufficient; friendly without getting all sloppy about it, and as obedient as he could be without having the fun knocked out of him. He was one of the boys and I could never get over thinking he was the smartest member of the gang. Gabe was a Border-Aussie, an obscure mixed breed known to be one-person dogs, but with enough room in their hearts for a "special friend." I was that friend. Vince said it was because I have a way with animals and I suppose that's true enough, but the pocketful of dog biscuits I always carried didn't hurt.

Gabe died a few years ago and Vince now has another dog, but there's no comparison. He'd promised his ailing mother-in-law that if anything happened he'd look after her little dog. Then she died and so, being an honorable man, Vince now has a ridiculous little thirteen-year-old shih tzu named Paris. We tried taking Paris fishing a few times, but she didn't care for it. Just as well because being seen with her was kind of embarrassing.

I didn't fish the lease this year until the middle of July. We had a fairly normal winter snowpack, but then April was unusually wet and May was the wettest on record, so by the first of June that alpine

29

peak that looks so romantic in wedding photos was still deep in snow and the so-called spring runoff lasted well into the middle of summer.

Some of us drove up there a few times in late June and early July to check the flow and water temperature, only to find that the former was always too high and the latter too low. Once we could just check the flow on a website, but the gauging station there blew out in a flood a few years ago and hasn't been replaced yet. I liked this old-timey business of going to the stream to see how it looked, something I didn't realize I'd begun to lose track of until I actually lost track of it. Even if you're just driving up for a quick look, you naturally bring wading boots in case you want to get in the water, and as long as you've got those, you might as well toss in a rod, reel, and fly box. Maybe you'll make a few casts even if the water is still too high and cold. Or maybe, since you're up there anyway, you'll drive to one of the other two tributaries in the area or the roadside lake with greenback cutthroats or the nearby tailwater. In this way, what could have been sixty seconds of gazing at a computer screen and clicking a mouse becomes a day in the mountains.

By the third week of July the water at the lease was clear and 51 degrees, but still running too high and fast. In other words, close enough for me and Vince to try it. Runoff is a fact of life here and everyone I know pushes through marginal conditions hoping to stretch the too-short post-runoff seasons these wet years allow us. Sometimes it's a bust, but now and then it works beautifully. That same summer, on a nearby stream that was even higher and colder, I managed to land only two trout all afternoon, but one of them was the biggest cutthroat I'd seen there in years. I'm convinced that if I'd waited for perfect conditions I'd have caught more fish, but I wouldn't have caught *that* one.

The lease fished well enough considering that much of it was still unfishable. (It's a lot to ask of a trout to swim all the way to the surface in fast current for a little dry fly, even if he can see it, and we hardly ever nymph-fish here, probably because we usually don't have to.) We picked up a few small trout here and there—not many, but enough to let us deliver a promising report—and then halfway up the riffle above the Rock Pool we saw a tall man in a tux and three women in matching long dresses walking across the bridge: young, trim, handsome people who wore their formal clothes as if they dressed like that every day.

So we hiked back to the truck and drove to the top of the lease to check the signs there for the first time that year. One was faded enough that it was getting hard to read at a distance and the other was bent double from an unsuccessful attempt to tear it down. Vince would have had his tools in the pickup, but we didn't have any new signs, so this would take a return trip after a stop at the hardware store. The water was coming down fast by then, so the stream could be fishing better by the time we got back.

I do think a few people poach here in the usual amateur way, which is to nip a little bit at each end. They'll be fishing up or downstream when they come to the signs and they'll stop to think about it. The water they can see looks pretty good. There's no one around. The owners are probably fat old plutocrats who never fish anyway, so what the hell? They wade on in, make a few casts, and maybe land an illicit trout or two. The water up ahead looks pretty good, too, but by now, being basically law-abiding people, they're beginning to feel nervous and guilty and they've made their point, so they turn around and leave. They may congratulate themselves for committing the perfect misdemeanor, but they might also be surprised that they didn't start hanging 20-inch trout the minute they cast a fly on forbidden water. At least that's how I used to do it.

If you do hook a decent-size trout here it will rarely be more than a foot long and it will probably turn out to be a brown, just like on the surrounding miles of public water. The brook trout are usually smaller—a 10-incher is a real nice fish—but they've always been my favorites, especially later in the year when they go into their spawning colors. They've always reminded me of Japanese miniatures that wouldn't be as striking if they were bigger, which doesn't mean I'm disappointed on the rare day when I land one that's 15 inches long.

Don't get me wrong, I'm as likely as anyone to travel long distances at great expense looking for big fish—including to Labrador and Quebec for giant native brook trout—but these mountain creeks are where I learned to fly-fish and even after a big trip up north I can reacquire the scale of things here in minutes.

I'm not alone in this. Once a famous, elderly fisherman dropped by a lodge in northern New Mexico where a friend of mine was guiding. This guy was one of those early jet-setters who'd been everywhere, caught everything, and whom you might suspect of being a little spoiled. My friend said that after a day or two of hauling in big, stocked trout, the old man got bored, took him aside, and said, "Don't suppose there's a creek around here with some little wild brookies?" It turns out there was. There almost always is.

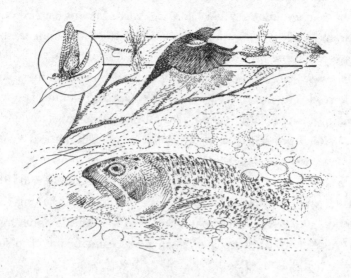

4.

GREEN DRAKES

I'm trying to remember if I was disappointed by my first Green Drake hatch. At the time—the late 1970s—fly shops, guides, and fishing writers all hyped the so-called super hatches so unmercifully that they virtually set you up to be disappointed. These were the Beatles concerts of fly-fishing, they said; all you had to do was get to the right place at the right time and you'd have a story to tell your grandchildren. That's provided you had the latest fly pattern, of course, which some of these folks were conveniently offering for sale.

Maybe "disappointed" is the wrong word. I was young the first time I made the pilgrimage to the Henry's Fork of the Snake River in Idaho for the Green Drakes, but not so young that I believed everything I heard. On the other hand, this was a famous hatch on the biggest and most famous spring creek in the Rocky Mountains, so I did have some cautious expectations.

That was almost forty years ago and what I remember most now is the crowd. The dirt parking lot at Mike Lawson's old fly shop was packed with cars bearing license plates from dozens of states and a few Canadian provinces; so many Winnebagos were parked in the field across the road that it looked like an aluminum subdivision, and the day after we pitched our tents there the KOA campground put a "FULL" sign out front. At mealtimes every table in the one café in town was taken and we sometimes had to wait on the porch for a seat. I never knew if this place had an actual name or not. The sign out front just said "EAT."

This was the most people I'd ever seen fishing in the same place at the same time. A few were locals exhibiting the strained patience common to residents of places where tourists congregate, but most were out-of-towners in for the big event: serious catch-and-release hatch-chasers who fished hard and well and who considered killing a trout to be the equivalent of murder, never mind the slot limit that allowed for one fish over 20 inches. One day a kid in his teens did kill a trout. It was an enormous rainbow—round as a watermelon and pushing 30 inches long—but when he innocently lugged the corpse over to the fly shop to show it off, the angry catch-and-release fishermen began to form a lynch mob. Finally Mike Lawson himself came out to defuse things. He looked at the fish, drawled, "Well, if I caught a trout that big, *I'd* keep it," and then sauntered back to his office.

The fashion at the time was to toss around Latin taxonomy as if you were more scientist than fisherman, so when a helpful streamside entomologist explained what had been going on with the hatches

I nodded knowingly, thanked him, and then later checked my copy of *Hatches* by Caucci & Nastasi to find out what the hell he was talking about. Mostly it was Green Drakes, sometimes interspersed with two sizes of Pale Morning Duns, plus spent caddis or rusty spinners in the evenings and ants or beetles for the solitary bank feeders.

The hot Drake pattern that year was an extended-body Paradrake made of olive-dyed deer hair. It was a killer pattern, but it was so fragile the sharp teeth of a few trout would shred the deer hair and make the fly unusable. We bought them by the handful at Lawson's, where they were kept in big fishbowls next to the cash register.

At first we weren't sure we'd be able to find a place to fish with all these people, but this was a big, wide, braided river that was easy to wade and lousy with trout, so it wasn't that hard to locate an unoccupied pod of risers. That's all it took. A few rising trout could keep you busy for hours, casting, mending, resting the fish when they got nervous, trying different flies, reducing tippet size, and finally just standing there trying to puzzle out the clue you'd missed. People said the trout went crazy over these big mayflies, but the fish I saw were feeding as sedately as grazing cattle. A little craziness would have been a relief.

We did catch fish, but it wasn't easy—for us or anyone else. Still, we caught enough to learn that it was the 16- to 18-inch rainbows that were hotter, faster, and jumped higher, while the big boys over 20 inches conserved their strength by staying in the water and fighting with their weight. And there were a few that just spooled us, boring off unstoppably until they had so much line out that the pull of the current against the belly of it broke the leader. We could while away whole evenings in camp wondering how big some of those trout must have been.

One day we were fishing a spot on the Harriman State Park water where a tongue of current ran past the end of a sweeper and noticed a blackbird that had perched on one of the last exposed twigs to pick passing mayflies off the water. That seemed pretty ingenious and we were watching the bird when there was a tremendous, splashy boil right under it and the bird flapped off in a loud, awkward panic. What we thought we saw was a huge trout try to eat a blackbird and nearly succeed, although in retrospect it seems more likely that the bird and the fish reached for the same mayfly at the same time and scared the hell out of each other. But we liked our first impression so much that we still tell the story that way, and the fish, which we never actually saw, has now grown to world record proportions.

I couldn't have been too disappointed because some friends and I made regular trips back there until the troubles began. Dewatering, anchor ice, siltation, and so on, all mostly collateral damage in the war between trout and potatoes that, in Idaho at least, potatoes usually win. There were some bad seasons, but the fishing gradually came back and it's still a wonderful river, now looked after by The Henry's Fork Foundation. Fishermen under forty say it's back to being as good as it ever was, while some over fifty say it'll never be the same again.

We took to fishing the Green Drakes on the Frying Pan River back home in Colorado, which had the advantage of being a five-hour drive instead of twelve or fourteen. The crowds were smaller, but so was the river, so the effect was about the same. We'd find the head of the hatch by driving upriver until we started seeing knots of guided fishermen, then we'd turn around and drive back downstream to the first vacant water and fish there. Sometimes Drakes would still be petering off in smaller numbers, and even if they weren't, the trout remembered them and could sometimes be convinced to eat our flies.

We also learned to avoid the big named pools where guides and clients congregated and to work the pocket water. There weren't always as many fish, but sometimes there were surprisingly big ones holding in little seams and eddies where getting a good drift involved some tricky casting and line mending. I remember pondering some of those casts for the longest time, planning elaborate presentations that sometimes worked better in theory than in practice. It had to be right the first time because dragging a fly over one of those trout could send him to the bottom to pout for the next half hour.

One of the most dependable flies there was the Frying Pan Green Drake as tied by my friend A. K. Best. When this pattern first came out some people said its proportions were all wrong—the body was too fat and the wings were too long—but the trout loved them and for years A.K. couldn't tie them fast enough to satisfy his customers who'd decided the wings weren't too long after all.

The Pan was also the first river where I tried Rene Harrop's Green Drake Biot Emerger, a fly that was developed on the Henry's Fork but somehow eluded me when I fished there. This is a simple, soft-hackled wet fly that never got very popular because at the time fishermen wanted flies that were more elaborately realistic. I did well with it fished as a dropper behind a dry fly, swung downstream wet fly-style, or greased and floated as a cripple. This fly is so sparse and simple that there isn't a lot for a trout to find fault with, while more complicated flies can look too much like a hard sell.

For a few years we fished the Green Drake hatch on a small river in Wyoming where the timing had to be flawless. The best stretch for Drakes ran through property so private it was considered trespassing to so much as drop an anchor, let alone set foot on dry land, so you had to float it. The trouble was that the Drake hatch came off just as the stream was dropping into summer flows that were too low to float even a small raft. Some years there was as little as a week or ten days when the hatch was on while the river was still navigable and we'd never have hit this right if not for a friend who guided a bigger river nearby and kept an eye on it. He'd call when he could arrange a day off during the hatch and there was never much notice, but we always managed to work it in.

I remember this as the best Green Drake hatch I ever fished. It's not so much that the hatch itself was heavier or that there were more and bigger fish as that we had it to ourselves. I tried out a Green Drake pattern there that I was working on at the time. Like most so-called new flies, it was a hodgepodge of other people's ideas combined on my own hook—like a medley of recognizable old songs—but I liked the looks of it and thought it might work. It did, but I knew it wasn't a fair test because these trout hadn't yet been trained to be shy of artificial flies.

Of course some locals and other guides knew about this hatch, but the timing was tricky enough that for a while at least we never ran into any of them. And then we started to; first one other boat, then two or three and so on. Some guides had floated friends who then came back with their own boats and friends, and then those friends did the same and word steadily spread. For a while there was an effort to keep this a secret, but eventually folks started running guided trips.

But the stream was too small for all that traffic and eventually there were full-blown boat jams and entire days spent breathing other people's exhaust. I'd fished crowded water before without batting an eye and probably will again, but on a stream you once had to yourself it's hard to get that sense of lost solitude out of your head. So when our friend gave up guiding for a regular job the rest of us moved on, too, in the same way that you'll lose track of someone who's gotten so busy making a living he can't spare the time to go fishing anymore.

Another guide I know showed me and a mutual friend the Green Drake hatch on a river just north of here. I knew there was a Drake hatch there and I'd even heard it was best on the long bench of land that runs past Sleeping Elephant Mountain, but I hadn't put in the time and effort it would have taken to work out the access through the patchwork of private land.

There are a lot of summer cabins through here and the Drakes come off in July when those cabins are occupied. I'd been tempted to fudge the boundaries and take my chances on the antique notion that fishermen operate outside the usual rules, but that really *is* an antique notion now and nothing ruins a day of fishing quicker than a run-in with an irate landowner. Sometimes the only thing that saves you from getting punched in the face is that you're out in the water and the guy doesn't want to get his Birkenstocks wet. He might threaten to call the cops, but you both know the cops won't drive all the way up here for this kind of minor skirmish, and even if they did, you'd be long gone by the time they arrived. Still, all that yelling leaves a bad taste in your mouth.

We launched our friend's raft at an improvised put-in and dawdled for a while, casting caddis flies. He'd been guiding this hatch for weeks now, had its timing wired, and wanted to save the best water for when the Drakes came off. We saw the first few flies on the water at about half past noon, a little behind schedule, but not so late that we'd started to worry. I was wearing the kind of loosely woven straw hat that makes a good bug net, so when one flew close enough to the boat I snatched it and had a look for old time's sake. It was big for a mayfly—almost an inch long nose to tail—with a smoky olive body, tall gray wings, head and tail elevated in an oddly regal posture as if the bug were proud of itself for being so handsome. Trout love mayflies because they're loaded with protein and easy to catch. Fishermen love them because they're pretty in an overbuilt, Victorian way, and we like the big ones because they're so easy to see on the water.

By the time a few fish had begun to rise I'd tied on the Drake pattern I first tried out in Wyoming with a Harrop Emerger on a dropper for good measure. Most of the trout I caught wanted a dead drift, but a few liked a slight upstream twitch to convince them that these flies were actually alive and therefore edible. And a few that didn't buy either of those would grab the emerger if I tightened the line and let it swing a little at the end of the drift. And that about exhausted my repertoire of tricks.

It was a good hatch with plenty of flies and it had been on for weeks, so the fish not only expected the bugs, but were looking forward to them. They didn't exactly go crazy—I've yet to see trout actually go crazy over this hatch—but some were eager enough to let themselves be fooled.

A week or so later a friend from France stayed with me for a few days on his way to Montana. This is a man who's so enthralled with the American West that he started a publishing company in Paris specializing in translations of western authors, which, in turn, lets him come out here for a month or so every year to travel around the Rocky Mountains in a rental car meeting with writers. And it just so happens that most of those meetings take place on trout streams.

The first day I took him to a mountain creek in the nearby national park that had been fishing well that year and that's also one of the prettiest places I know. It was a chilly, rainy day with no one else on the water and we caught fish easily on nondescript dry flies.

On the drive home we talked about where we'd go the next day. I ran down some possibilities, but when I mentioned that I knew a place where there might still be some Green Drakes hatching he jumped on it. He said he'd always dreamed of fishing a Green Drake hatch with A. K. Best flies because he'd been reading about both for years. It seemed providential that Mike Clark's bamboo rod shop in

Lyons—one of the few places where you can still buy flies tied by A. K.—was just ten minutes out of our way, so we stopped and he bought a handful of Drake patterns—enough for a day of fishing, plus a few extras to take home as souvenirs.

We got on the water at about ten thirty the next morning. The front from the day before had socked in and it was another uncharacteristically cool, gray day threatening rain. Perfect summer dry fly weather. We staked out a big, luxurious pool and saw the first Drakes popping off within half an hour. We fished the run slowly, taking turns as we worked our way up to the sweet spot at the head. My friend caught his first trout ever on a Green Drake, then his second, and third, and so on.

It took us a couple of hours to finally put that pool down and then we worked downstream through some pocket water to the first no-trespassing sign. There were a few straggling Drakes coming off, but the fish weren't interested. Then we went upstream through a long reach of riffly water and saw no Drakes at all.

I assumed that someone would have grabbed our pool by then, but when we walked back downriver more than an hour later it was still vacant and some fish had started rising again. We got a few more trout on Drakes before they finally petered out and finished off with a few more on Pale Morning Duns. Then the rain that had been threatening all day hit in an afternoon downpour and that was it.

On the drive home with the windshield wipers slapping, my friend went on and on about the stark beauty of the Rocky Mountains: this river valley in particular, which he'd never seen before, as well as all the places he *had* seen. Compared to Europe the American West still seems wild and unpopulated and he's charmed by everything here in the way you can only be with a country that's not your own. The mind-cleansing open spaces, the craggy scenery, all the public water you can fish, the rough politeness of the people—so unlike Parisians, he said—and even domestic wine. "Why buy French wine in America?" He said, "It's a waste of money."

It did me good to hear this testimonial. I do love this region, but there are days when the loveliness of it fades into a day-to-day background of deadlines, money troubles, and broken water heaters. I'd shown my friend where to catch some trout, but he'd done me a bigger favor in return by seeing with fresh eyes what I'd gotten used to. I felt like a schlub who'd been taking his wife for granted until someone else made a pass at her.

That night at dinner he told some of my friends that he'd had two fine days on the water and that if I ever decided to do it professionally I'd be the best fishing guide in Colorado. They shot me disbelieving looks, but were polite enough not to say anything.

5.

FISH DOGS

After an hour's boat ride from the nearest town we were still a hundred yards from the dock at a fishing camp in Alaska when Doug shouted, "Look, a yellow Lab!" Funky old cabins, johnboats, floatplanes, and a week of fishing ahead of us and what excites the guy is the sight of a dog. Me, too.

Some of the guides were ambling down to the dock in no big hurry to lug the new clients' duffels and rod cases to their cabins, but the Lab came at a full gallop, ears flapping like wings. This was Duke, who went through the new fishermen one by one, making a mental note of who seemed indifferent, who gave him a cursory pat, and who got down on one knee to rub his ears and let themselves be licked like Doug and I did. You could literally see him moving us into the column labeled "pushovers."

One of Duke's official duties at the lodge—maybe his *only* official duty—was to meet every arriving boat and floatplane and his level of enthusiasm was calibrated to who was on board. (Using that spooky sixth sense dogs have, he somehow always knew in advance.) He was always happy enough to see me and Doug and would sometimes follow us to our cabin to see if we'd saved him a treat from lunch. And one day when we had to wait for hours for the weather to break so we could fly out to a salmon river, Duke kept us company with his chin on his paws, channeling our boredom.

But his real favorites that week were the two young daughters of a returning client, ages twelve and fourteen. Whenever they were in camp, Duke was always with them, trotting along as eager and attentive as a puppy. Early one morning I glanced out the bathroom window and happened to see the younger of the girls open their cabin door a crack and out stepped Duke, looking sleepy, sheepish, and pleased with himself.

At breakfast I asked the girl if Duke had been spending his nights with them.

"Yup," she said.

"In bed?" I asked.

"Of course."

Not all camp dogs are as sloppily friendly as Duke. There are one-man dogs that are tight with their owners, but uninterested in strangers; dogs that are too busy with their self-imposed duties as bear lookout or lemming hunter to bother much with people; and even the occasional wolf hybrid with the kind of menacing dignity that rules out fraternization. But even those that are standoffish will tumble for a piece of bacon slipped from the breakfast table.

Anyone who says you can't buy love has never spent time around dogs.

Camp dogs may or may not be fishing dogs, but even if they are it's an unwritten rule that letting them go out with clients is too much of a gamble. Some don't want a dog underfoot, others say they do but are just being polite, and even those who think fishing with the dog would be fun can change their minds when the dog in question steps on and breaks their rod, goes after a big fish they're trying to land, or commits any of the dozens of other innocent mistakes a fun-loving mutt can make in the heat of the moment.

In fact, a really good fishing dog is a rare and valuable animal. When it comes to fishing, most dogs have failings and idiosyncrasies that their owners have learned to appreciate or at least live with, but that others find unforgivable.

For instance, Bella, another yellow Lab, thinks fishermen are only there to locate and hook a fish so she knows where it is, but that it's then up to her to retrieve it. She's even been known to dive out of a drift boat and swim after a fish that's being played. The first time I saw her in action I'd hooked a small brook trout, heard my friend downstream yell, "Bella! *No!*" and in less time than it takes to tell, Bella was in the water and had the little trout in her mouth. I think my friend let this happen once so I'd understand the magnitude of the problem. After that, one of us would fish while the other physically restrained the dog—and Bella is a big, strong girl who doesn't appreciate being restrained.

Now, it's easy to say that Bella misunderstands fishing, but maybe it's just that dogs comprehend things in literal ways that, if we were objective, we'd find it hard to argue with. From Bella's point of view, we human fly fishermen are inefficiently catlike; pointlessly toying with our prey using light tippets and small flies instead of going in for the quick kill the way any self-respecting canine would. Or as

Bella herself might say, "For Christ's sake let me grab it before it gets away!"

Sometimes it's possible to train a dog to leave the fish alone, only to have that pent-up enthusiasm squeeze out in an unexpected direction. Once I fished the Missouri River with a guide who had one of those generic ranch dogs you see all over the mountain West: small, quick, agile, and high-strung with a heritage that reflects blue heeler, border collie, Australian shepherd, and whatever else happened to get over the fence. The problem with these dogs is that they're bred for herding and when you deprive them of their rightful livelihoods, they'll invent new and sometimes pointless jobs that they can do with the same headlong intensity.

This dog had decided it had to bark continuously and piercingly from the moment a fish was hooked until it was in the net. At first it was funny—look how excited she gets!—but this wasn't happy barking; it was hysterical, breathless caterwauling complete with flying slobber and bulging eyes. The fishing was good that week and there were plenty of big trout that took some time to land, so by the end of the first day I had a headache and by day three I was idly wondering if there was a way to drown the dog and make it look like an accident.

But I can't blame the breed because one of the best dogs I ever fished with was also a herding dog, a pure-bred blue heeler as near as I could tell. He lived on a ranch that had leased its big, spring-fed lake to a guide service that planted it with large rainbow trout, and since these dogs are quick studies, he'd immediately figured out not only how fishing worked, but how he could participate in a helpful way. His name may or may not have been Buddy, but that's what the guides called him.

As you walked the shore of the lake looking for cruising trout, Buddy would walk a few paces ahead, doing the same thing. When he spotted one, he'd go into a deep crouch with his ears cocked forward and his stub of a tail vibrating like a tuning fork. (It wasn't a classic English setter point, but you got the idea.) He was happy to wait patiently while you hooked, played, and landed a fish and then step in for a quick sniff before you released it. If a fish didn't take, he'd shrug philosophically and move on, but if you missed a strike or had a fish on and lost it, he'd turn and give you a withering look. In fact Buddy was the only dog I ever met who could roll his eyes.

You'd think a six-foot-tall fisherman wearing polarized sunglasses would be able to see fish better than a dog that was no more than twenty inches off the ground, but you'd be wrong. The best I could ever do was spot a fish at the same time Buddy did, but never before.

I heard that a few years later Buddy came to a bad end. When he wasn't fishing he had a thing for chasing cars, but he wasn't as young and agile as he used to be and one day he took a wrong step: another case study in the dangers of obsession.

Moose is a black Lab who, at age ten, is still trim and muscular, but sports a gray Vandyke on his muzzle that creates the illusion of dignity until you get to know him. He's hunted and fished all his life with his photographer owner and fully comprehends the ins and outs of both sports, as well as the significant difference between a shotgun and a fly rod.

When he's out fishing, he plods along gamely, rarely running ahead or lagging behind without what he judges to be a good reason. (You can't expect a dog to be better behaved than his owner.) Moose aspires to be a good fishing dog and he knows the rules, but he also understands that those rules are sometimes negotiable. For instance, a good fish dog stays out of the water when people are fishing, but once on a stream in Wisconsin we were watching his owner casting to a pool upstream when Moose walked over to the water, put a foot in, and gave me a look over his shoulder. I said,

"Okay, but stay right there." He slipped into the water like an otter, swam in place facing the current for a few minutes as if he were on a treadmill, and then got out, shook off, and sat back down next to me with a look that said, "Thanks, I needed that." As the author William Bennett didn't exactly say, "It takes a firm hand (or a Labrador retriever) to bend rules well."

And, true to his breed, Moose is an incurable food whore. Sometimes I think he likes to go fishing only because he knows fishermen eventually stop for lunch. He doesn't beg in any of the conventional ways—there's no pawing, nudging, whining, or groveling—but when you're eating he goes into a state of existential crisis over whether or not he'll get a bite and he can stare at you with enough intensity to make your sandwich vibrate.

Labs in general are capable of high-level conceptual thinking when it comes to food. I used to know a Lab named Oso—short for *Oso Negro,* or black bear. Every morning when his owner took him into the fly shop where he presided as shop dog, Oso would disappear for twenty minutes or so. His owner assumed he was just out doing what dogs do—wandering around the neighborhood sniffing things and peeing on carefully chosen objects—but in fact he'd walk over to the drive-up window at the bank and bark until the teller sent out a dog biscuit in the tray.

It occurs to me that every good fishing dog I ever met was at least middle-aged if not older—or about the age I am now in dog years. It can take years of trial and error to figure out how things work, but smart dogs, like smart humans, finally reach an emotional cruising altitude where they're far from perfect, but still able to function adequately in the world as they know it. Or not, and *if* not, they don't get to go fishing anymore.

Tucker, yet another yellow Lab, was downright old when I met him. He was a little overweight and arthritic from a working life spent in duck blinds—a job he'd retired from several years before—but he still liked to go fishing. He'd lie on the bank while his owner fished, in a patch of sunlight if he could find one. Sometimes he'd stand up and watch when his owner caught a fish; other times he'd just lift his head off his paws and wag his tail. On a slow day he might fall asleep. Afterward he'd trudge home to eat a big bowl of dog food and take a long nap, ravenous and exhausted from his workout.

Bear, a golden retriever who spends his summers at a fishing lodge in Labrador, isn't elderly yet, although he's slowed down some and has an old dog's gray muzzle and those eyes that, in quiet moments, seem to be staring at something you can't see. Bear sticks as close to his owner as he can: right at his knee when possible or perched attentively on a nearby rock if Dad wades too deep. Bear understands where the fish come from—if not exactly how—so he intently watches the drift of a dry fly or the swing of a streamer and wags his tail when the line comes tight. There's no barking or other theatrics. He's happy because his owner is happy; it's no more complicated than that.

Bear had a bad spell a few years ago when his lifelong companion—another golden, named Georgia—died of cancer and Bear went into such a deep depression that his owner thought he might not survive. (It happens; a dog is fully capable of dying of a broken heart.) So my friend did the only thing he could and bought Bear a puppy, another golden named Sam. Within a week these two were inseparable—sleeping together, chewing on each other's faces—and Bear had some of the spring back in his step, proving once again that no one can resist a golden retriever puppy, including another golden.

These dogs live charmed lives, spending their winters on a farm in Vermont and their summers at a fishing lodge in Labrador where they fly in floatplanes as casually as most dogs ride in pickups. In both places they're surrounded by the kind of people who'll automatically pet any dog within reach, so they get all the attention they could want. I doubt either of them has ever worn a collar.

Bear still enjoys fishing, but he doesn't seem crazy about it. I think he likes to go because it's his job to be there and keep an eye on things. On the other hand, he does like to have a look at each fish his owner lands (but *only* those his owner lands; he couldn't care less about anyone else's fish) and when things are slow back at camp he'll wade into the lake and study the minnows that collect around his legs.

If there's one characteristic common to all fishing dogs, it's that they want to have a look at the fish, although they don't all do it in the same way.

Maggie, a small, slightly skittish yellow Lab, wants to see the fish, but not at a range closer than about two feet, as if she thinks they might bite. We've tried to explain to her that they're just lake squirrels, but she's not convinced.

Happy Trout ("Trout" for short) was a chocolate Lab who could disappear for hours at a time, but still show up unerringly whenever a steelhead was hooked. When the fish was landed he'd give it a harmless little nibble and then wander off again as soon as it was released to chase rabbits and roll in anything that smelled dead. He may have been more attentive on a trout stream, where there can be more action, but when it came to steelhead he understood that landing one was a momentous occasion, but that it didn't happen all that often.

And Zane, a Brittany spaniel who'd steal your seat in a drift boat as soon as you stood up to cast and refuse to give it back, would happily lick any west-slope cutthroat that was landed, but would literally turn up his nose at a rainbow. Did he come up with this on his own or was he just mimicking his owner's obvious preference? There's no way to know.

There really *is* no way to know, but I still wonder what dogs think about fishing. If I had to guess, I'd say that as predators they understand catching things for sport, as companions they understand getting to go along, and if it ever occurred to them to ask why, then "because it's fun" would be answer enough. The only thing that's clear is that dogs enjoy themselves with an uncomplicated purity we can only envy and I'd give a lot to spend a day in the mind of a good fishing dog—but before I did I'd want an ironclad guarantee that I could get back out again.

And then there's Humpy. I'm not sure it's fair to call him a fishing dog, but he *is* owned by a fishing couple and has been around fish camps all his life. I don't know where he came from, but if I had to guess I'd say he was already with the woman my friend now lives with and was a nonnegotiable part of the deal.

The thing is—and there's no kind way to say this—Humpy is a white miniature poodle. Being greeted at an otherwise rough-and-tumble steelhead camp by this fuzz ball can make you question the wisdom of the trip, but most people get past that once they get to know him. For one thing, he's always had a voracious sexual appetite. (A friend once famously said that Humpy was not named after the fly pattern.) For another, he's fearlessly in touch with his inner wolf to the point of being suicidal. In fact he may be alive today only because I once stopped him from attacking two large pit bulls on the Klickitat River. And he was mad at me for doing it.

Humpy has now lived to an unbelievably old age, and although he's no less ridiculous, he's become weirdly venerable, sort of like Yoda. When I told a friend recently that Humpy was still alive at age eighteen, my friend asked, "How can you tell?" Good question. It's true that Humpy's joints no longer bend and that he's now mostly deaf and blind and sometimes barks at things that aren't there, but he seems to be aware of his surroundings in an intuitive way and enjoys being around rivers and fishermen. If nothing else, he can still smell both.

In his later years, Humpy has begun to remind me of Keith Richards, the venerable guitar player with the Rolling Stones who still kicks it out admirably at an age when so many rockers of his era have either died or been decommissioned. Richards and Humpy are both examples of longevity against steep odds and they both seem to have achieved the kind of goofy blissfulness that only comes with time and acceptance. Humpy still sometimes stands with his blind eyes staring at nothing and his nose in the air, breathing in all the good stuff he can no longer see or hear. And once at a concert Richards lurched to the microphone like an animated corpse and said, "It's good to be here . . . Fuck, man, it's good to be *anywhere.*"

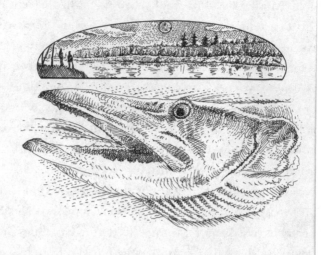

6.

MUSKY

I thought it was an eloquent juxtaposition of scale that the str
I was casting for muskies in northern Wisconsin were the sar
as the trout I'd been catching back home in Colorado just a fe
earlier. Sometimes fishing tackle alone tells half the story and
the guide hands you an 11-weight fly rod with a wire leader ar
the size of a squirrel, you begin to get a sense of how the n
days might shake out.

These were guide flies in the sense of being nicely tied ar
a few subtle touches that may not have been absolutely ne
but still a lot simpler than some and therefore faster to tie an

expendable, although if you snag one you'll go and get it if that's at all possible. Musky flies—like those for other fish that are notoriously hard to catch—can go off the deep end as fly tiers try to use imaginary anatomical features and unearthly color combinations to trip an elusive predatory switch in the dim brains of their quarry. The flies can be works of art, but there may be something else at work here, too. Some musky wonks have gone so far as to tie flies that look like ducklings, complete with cute little yellow beaks. They probably work, but also double as testimony that these fish are big and murderous enough to eat a duck.

This wasn't my first experience with muskies. When I'd gone smallmouth bass fishing on the Flambeau, Chippewa, and Namekagon Rivers in past years I'd learned to tie my bass bugs onto 65-pound PowerPro shock tippets to keep the muskies from biting them off. (At the time a Whitlock Swimming Frog sold for $6.95.) In the course of those trips I landed a few smaller muskies—not quite by accident, but not entirely on purpose, either—and saw a big one grab a bass a friend was playing and bite it nearly in half. None of these fish were especially large as muskies go, but if they weren't a qualitative step up from a two-pound smallmouth bass, they were at least something entirely different: the big fish that eats the smaller fish you've been catching, sometimes right off your hook.

So when Bob White asked me to join the musky trip he puts together every fall I realized that this was something I'd been wanting to do and that this would be the way to do it. Bob is a sporting artist with a shadow career as a fishing guide and a talent for organization. For this trip he'd put a small group of experienced anglers who were new to muskies together with some hard-core local musky guides, rented an old lodge on the Chippewa River that's rumored to have once been a speakeasy, and billed the event as "Musky Madness."

Furthermore, to spare clients the daunting expense of buying the specialized rods, lines, wire leaders, and flies they'd need, Bob and the guides supplied the tackle, so all you had to bring were waders, warm clothes, and a raincoat. It was too easy to pass up and, for that matter, Bob is one of those friends I don't get to see often enough, and life is too short to either fish with people you don't like or to not fish with people you do.

One of the guides, Russ Gontarek, picked me up at the airport in Minneapolis on a rainy afternoon and we escaped the city together in the beginnings of a wet rush hour. Russ was coming right from his day job and was still wearing a tie, which reminded me of an old riddle:

"What do you call a fishing guide wearing a necktie?" I asked.

"What?"

"The defendant."

It was about a three-hour drive from Minneapolis to Ojibwa County in Wisconsin, during which the roads got narrower, the traffic got thinner, the trees got thicker, and the towns got smaller and farther apart until finally they became self-contained instead of just places to sleep for those who worked elsewhere. These villages aren't at all timeless or backward—they have all the modern conveniences, from the Internet to methamphetamines—but the pace is more human. In the city you can't get your errands done because of crowds and traffic; up here locals can't get their errands done because everywhere they go someone wants to stop and talk. Even strangers just dropping by for gas and coffee can get drawn into long conversations about fishing, the coming deer season, or the recent sighting of a wolf.

I grew into my early teens nearby in Minnesota, and although I've been known to listen to Garrison Keillor, I don't get overly nostalgic about my youth in the upper Midwest until I find myself back there. It doesn't exactly feel like a homecoming—I moved away more than half a century ago and haven't thought about moving back—but there's still an overwhelming sense of recognition. More than anything it's those flat Middle American voices—still sometimes brightened by the Swedish lilt that fades a little more with each generation—as well as the attitude that goes with them: long-standing rural pride seasoned with a dash of defensiveness. I remember a certain kind of midwesterner who'd say things like, "Look, I know the score; I didn't just fall off the turnip truck," which meant that whether he knew the score or not, he actually *had* just fallen off the turnip truck in some symbolic way.

Neither of us had ever been to this lodge before and we were up in the woods now, where the map function on Russ's cell phone—deprived of cross streets and numbered addresses—didn't seem to know where it was. We pulled in at one large frame lodge building that looked promising, but then saw in the wan, late afternoon light that it was abandoned and woebegone with boarded-up windows and a sagging roof. But then a little farther down the same road we came to another big, rambling place with lights on in the windows, drift boats parked in the yard, and a small crowd of people who could only be fishermen loitering outside. We didn't see the Chippewa River Lodge sign until we'd already turned in.

Muskies are large fish by nature. If you want to keep one, it has to be at least 40 inches long just to be legal, but if you hope to impress anyone with a trophy, you'll have to aim higher. A casual survey of the restaurants and bars in this part of the country suggests that a fish 50-plus inches long and with some girth is about the minimum size you could mount on a wall without risking ridicule. And for added perspective you can always drive over to the Moccasin Bar in Hayward to see the mounted 67½-pound musky caught by Cal

Johnson in the 1940s. This fish isn't really as big as a canoe, but in the confines of the small, low-ceilinged tavern, that's how it looks and the sight of it could save you a fortune in taxidermy bills.

Any angler with a specialty naturally thinks his chosen fish is far and away the coolest thing that swims and he'll go on and on about it with his voice gradually rising, his hand gestures getting broader, and his eyes taking on an unhealthy-looking shine. This usually happens on the first night in camp and it's possible to get pretty pumped up with advice, which is all good, but hard to keep straight. One thing is clear from the beginning, though. As with other famously difficult fish, the work ethic it takes to get one of these things to the boat becomes a point of pride and there are no meat buckets in musky fishing, just hard-won individual fish. It also occurs to you that although this isn't especially high-concept stuff, it's also not something you're likely to get right on your first try.

Once you're out on the river the guide will choose your fly, tell you where to cast, and coach you on the retrieve, so the emphasis is on hook setting, which is where beginners invariably screw the pooch. A musky looks like a short, fat snake with the face of a goose with teeth (something only a fisherman could love) and those wide, strong, bony jaws studded with fangs can hold a fly so securely that it won't move enough on the set for the hook point to sink. I'd been the victim of this on some of those bass trips when I'd set as hard as I thought I should on a musky and played it more or less confidently for thirty seconds or more, only to have the fish decide this thing was more trouble than it was worth and simply open its mouth and release the fly.

The trick, they say, is to wait until you feel the weight of the fish (there'll be no mistake about that) and then with the rod still pointed at the fly, strip set by yanking as hard as you can with your line hand and then set just as hard with the rod. And I mean hard. To make the point one of the guides said, "First you try to break the line; then you try to break the rod." Some fall back on the traditional advice that you should set hard four or five times in quick succession; others say once or twice is good if you do it hard enough, but no one claims either method is foolproof. This comes easier to saltwater fishermen who are used to strip-setting hard on big fish, but not so much to us trout guys whose muscle memory insists on lifting the rod tip just smartly enough to sink a size 16, light wire hook.

Musky fishermen describe these fish as moody, brooding, elusive, and unpredictable, as if their reticence about biting flies were evidence of a character flaw, but I think a large part of it is that you never know where they are. As big as some of them get, you'd think you'd be able to spot them, but they're magnificently camouflaged with mud-colored backs and cryptic markings on their flanks that make them invisible even in just a few feet of clear water. (People do see them from time to time, but usually only when they move.) So you're reduced to systematically working the slack currents with structure like deadfalls, brush piles, and rubble bottoms or potholes in riffles where muskies like to lurk and, with nothing more to go on, just hoping for the best.

Something else that makes these fish seem moody is their preference for large prey. Like any other apex predator, they'll eat whatever they can get if it comes to that (wolves eat more mice than they do caribou) but they're really out for something on the order of a large sucker or a baby muskrat. A musky is less like a trout that'll eat hundreds of mayflies in a day, and more like a lion that eats an antelope and then sleeps for a week.

Given this fish's behavioral profile, you assume that most of the muskies that see your fly just ignore it until it goes away, although there's no way to know that for sure. The ones that don't ignore it will usually do one of two things: they'll either strike as suddenly and unexpectedly as a cobra or they'll follow the fly like a curious puppy, sometimes right to the boat, and you can't always see that happening. So you learn to figure-8 the fly when it's still a rod's length from the boat on every retrieve, sticking the rod tip underwater to make the fly dive and climb and speeding it up on the turns so the fish will think it's getting away and lunge. Maybe. If there's even a fish there. Which there usually isn't. On the morning of the first day you do this with a sense of great expectation; by lunchtime, if you haven't gotten a follow, it becomes a rote maneuver.

Getting a curious but hesitant follower to take the fly calls for creativity under pressure. I heard a story from one of the guides about Gabe Schubert, whom I fished with later in the trip. Gabe saw a large musky following his fly to the boat and went into the figure-8, but however much he changed the depth, direction, and speed of the fly, the fish shadowed it, but wouldn't strike. Finally, in desperation, he stopped the fly—which they say you should never do—stood it up vertically in the water and wiggled it with the rod tip, and then picked it up and slapped it back down on the surface, at which point the musky ate it.

The story ended there and I never learned if he hooked or landed the fish or how big it was, but that wasn't the point. The point was the spectacle of skill and intuition it took to induce the strike. It's because of minor miracles like this that Gabe has come to be known in some circles as "Musky Jesus," a nickname he told me he doesn't care for.

And then there's the whole lunar angle. Musky fanatics believe that no matter what else is happening with weather, stream flow, water clarity, and temperature, these fish bite best under a full or new moon with smaller bumps in the action at the first and last quarters. This is such an article of faith with some that they plan their fishing trips accordingly and some of these guys are gone so often during the full moon that their wives and girlfriends have begun to suspect that they're werewolves.

The moon business sounds like superstition to nonbelievers, but there's statistical proof. Two musky fishing scientists in Wisconsin (where else?) pored over hundreds of thousands of archived catch records covering forty-three years, correlated the time and date of each catch with moon phase, and found that, sure enough, if you fish at the right time in the lunar cycle your chances of catching a musky increase by 5 percent. That may not seem like much, but if you knew what you were doing, a dependable 5 percent edge at the race track or in the stock market could make your fortune.

So that first night at the lodge we talked muskies for hours (or the guides talked and we listened) and in the morning we launched on the Flambeau and proceeded to keep our meat wet, the phrase a musky guide uses when he means you should keep your fly in the water. Relentlessness is important because muskies are known as "the fish of a thousand casts" and even someone trying to sell you on a guided trip will admit that a follow or two and maybe an eat constitutes a pretty good day of musky fishing. Then again, the night before, someone encouragingly said that they'd done the math and it actually worked out to only be about 675 casts on average between strikes.

True or not, I didn't know what to do with that information. Does a flubbed cast count the same as a perfect one? If you cast and re-trieve furiously in order to get to 675 casts sooner, do your odds im-prove? It's probably best to just bear down, put in your time, and try to master the cast and retrieve.

I spent an hour or so the first morning working out how to cast a foot-long fly that looked like it had taken an entire buck tail and part of a rooster to tie. I found that I actually could keep a quarter pound of wet hair airborne through a back cast or two, but it didn't seem like something I could keep up for days without blowing out the tendons in my shoulder and elbow and making myself useless.

So, on the guide's advice I resorted to the time-honored water haul. After the required figure-8s at the end of the retrieve I'd flip the big fly behind me, shooting a few extra rod lengths of line and letting the fly land on the surface. Then I'd use the surface tension of the water as an anchor for the forward cast. Viewed objectively, an angler performing a water haul looks like he's trying to recover from a mistake, but as clunky as it looks, it's damned efficient and you can keep it up for hours.

I blew a strike that day in the usual amateur way. I'd been reminding myself on each cast to strip instead of strike, but when a fish exploded on my fly, my arm automatically raised the rod tip even as my mind shouted, "No, no, no!" There was a single hard yank followed by a slack line, a tremendous boil of water and spray, and the fish was gone. Then, with nothing useful left to say, all three of us in the boat observed a moment of embarrassed silence.

Sometime later Bob hooked a musky that measured 42 inches and landed it after a short but appallingly violent battle. It was essentially a big muscle with lots of teeth designed for speed and concealment and it was amazing to see a thing like that lifted helplessly out of the water in broad daylight. Bob handled the fish confidently, but he was careful to keep his fingers away from the business end.

Not long after that I landed one that was just shy of the benchmark 40-inch minimum, but still a yard-long fish I couldn't turn up my nose at. One of the guys took a photo of it and the three of us leaned in to look at an image of the fish on a two-inch screen even as I still held the actual, nondigital musky in the water at our feet. It was a distinctly twenty-first-century moment.

We were not only fishing under a full moon that week (another example of Bob's knack for planning) but there was a total eclipse on one of our nights there, so we all piled outside after supper to watch it. The moon was floating above the tall white pines along the Chippewa River, scudding out of fast-moving clouds often enough for a good, clear view. This was predicted to be a blood moon, but at the crucial moment when the shadow of the earth completely covered the moon, it turned a kind of dusty rose color that was too delicately pretty to make me think of spilled blood. I thought that as a painter Bob would be able to name the color, but when I looked for him he was deep in conversation about something with two of the guides and by the time he was free I'd forgotten about it.

I also wondered if this rare astronomical event would have any effect on the 5 percent advantage of a full moon. No telling, although musky fishing statisticians somewhere in Wisconsin are no doubt crunching the numbers as we speak.

Late the next day I was retrieving another one of countless uneventful casts and went into the obligatory figure-8s at the boat, straining in the low light to spot a large shape following the fly and not seeing anything. But then when I lifted the fly for the next cast there was the briefest instant, like the flash of a camera, when I was staring straight into the open maw of an enormous musky that I didn't know was there until it was too late. I didn't think the fish ever actually had the fly, but Gabe was on the oars that day and said he'd seen the rod bend briefly. I don't remember feeling anything, but maybe there was just too much information for me to absorb at a split second's notice. Anyway, whatever happened, the fish was there and gone and that was that, and there was nothing I could do about it. It was a chilly fall afternoon with the leaves changing, the current whispering, and a pale moon in a daytime sky. The river seemed inscrutable, but alive with possibility.

And so it goes. The big one that gets away has always been an amusing cliché to people who don't fish, but to those of us who do, it's the stuff of sleeplessly staring at a dark bedroom ceiling wondering why you didn't just stay home to binge-watch *The Walking Dead.*

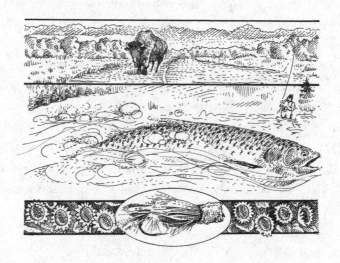

7.

BLACK HILLS

My friend Paul and I were fishing in the Black Hills in South Dakota at a place that was once so secret it was known to insiders as
Area 51, although now it's clearly marked as "Walk-in Fishing" with
a four-car parking lot and a sign warning of the combined hazards
of ticks, rattlesnakes, and poison ivy. On the drive in we'd passed an
enormous bull buffalo ambling up the center line of the two-lane
road with the nonchalant air of an animal that weighs a ton and goes
where it damned well pleases. We eased past him at the slowest
possible speed with the right wheels off the shoulder and the emer-
gency flashers going in case another car roared up behind us. I could

have reached out the open window and touched him—but didn't—
and even at point-blank range there was no sign that his big, brown
chestnut eye even registered our presence.

A little farther on I drove right past the place we were looking for
and didn't realize it until we came to the landmark that told us we'd
gone too far. (When the directions include the phrase, "You can't
miss it," I *can* miss it and usually do.)

This was a place where a narrow creek runs from a headwater
lake down a few miles of sparsely forested valley. There are small
ponds dammed up on the descending benches of land and a big
sprawling pond right at the parking lot. We'd planned to hike up the
trail, but trout were boiling on the bottom pond when we pulled in
and no one was fishing, so we decided to start there.

These fish were taking something just under the surface, leaving swirls that were sometimes broken by a tail or dorsal fin. There
weren't enough boils to let us pick out an individual trout and lead
it, so we blind-fished the water with slowly retrieved small nymphs.
Strikes came mostly from the shrinking band of shade along the east
shore in the form of indecisive tweaks that were easy to miss, slower
pulls that left time to set the hook, and the occasional hard yank
that was almost a sure thing as long as you didn't break off your fly.
These were all rainbows ranging from 10 or 11 inches long to a few
big boys pushing 16. We guessed that the smaller trout had been
freshly stocked earlier that year, while the big ones were holdovers
from last season. We wondered if there could be a few even older,
larger holdover trout in there and that kept us casting through the
morning until the day turned hot, the shade vanished, and the fishing petered off.

By the time we hiked up the valley we were into the heat of the
day and things had really slowed down. We picked up a few odd
trout fishing deep in the ponds, but in the creek it was nothing but

the ubiquitous 4-inch-long chubs that are nothing if not persistent and don't seem to care about high water temperature.

On the third pond we stopped to say hello to another fly fisherman who was only the second of our kind we'd seen since we got to the Black Hills. He was a poet named Michael who allowed as how the life of a poet in rural South Dakota wasn't an easy one, but he understood this would be part of the deal from the beginning and so didn't hold it against anyone. I guessed him in his late thirties or early forties. He held his fly rod thoughtlessly at his side like someone who's carried one all his life.

Farther up the valley we passed a man, his wife, and a wet cocker spaniel walking down the trail. The man was carrying a spinning rod and a stringer with two small brook trout from the headwater lake. That guy and the poet constituted the biggest crowd of fishermen we saw on the whole trip.

I'd been hearing about the trout fishing in the Black Hills for a few years by then, but always by way of second- or third-hand reports that were long on generalities but short on specifics. The only eyewitness account I'd heard was from Paul himself, who'd once driven through there on his way somewhere else, noticed all the small creeks, and stopped to fish for a day. He didn't remember much except that he'd picked a stream at random, caught a fat rainbow on his first cast, and that he was a day late getting where he was going.

So I was curious. Maybe it was the description I'd heard of this region as "an island of pine in an ocean of prairie" that made it sound like an undiscovered paradise, or the claims that although the fishing was pretty good by small stream standards, the great trout country of the Rocky Mountains began less than a day's drive to the west, so very few people ever stopped to fish the Black Hills. But whatever the reason for it, the thought of neglected trout fishing not that far from home was too much to resist.

We could have gone in cold—which is not a bad way to explore new water if you have the time—but I'd hedged our bet using a journalist's trick I picked up back in my newspaper days. I cold-called people at national forest, state park, and Fish, Game & Parks offices, half-listened as they recited the text from their websites more or less verbatim, and then politely asked if there was anyone who could go into more detail. In this way I gradually worked my way down the bureaucratic food chain from the people sitting behind desks to those driving pickup trucks with tools in the beds until finally a man said, "You know, you should talk to Keith."

"Let me guess," I said, "Keith is the guy on the crew who always has a fly rod in his car and goes fishing while everyone else is eating lunch."

"Yeah," the guy said. "You know him?"

I said, "No, but I know the type."

Keith Wintersteen turned out to have a background in fisheries and was now working as a naturalist with Fish, Game & Parks as well as being a kind of unofficial and possibly self-appointed booster for Black Hills trout fishing. On the phone he recited the tourist brochure stuff I'd heard so often I had it memorized, but as we talked more and hit it off in the way of fishermen with a ready-made universe of discourse, he began to let slip the kind of things we might not have rooted out on our own. So in September when Paul and I drove out across that ocean of prairie—which, coming from the southwest, includes parts of Colorado, Wyoming, Nebraska, and South Dakota—I had a crossword puzzle of tips, hints, and landmarks that I assumed would make more sense once we got the lay of the land.

This was a quiet drive, partly because the prairie viewed through a windshield is trance-inducing, but also because Paul has what a doctor described as "nodes" on his vocal cords that give his voice the volume and timbre of a breeze in dry leaves, so it couldn't rise above the road noise of my fifteen-year-old pickup. (When he's fishing, he carries a whistle so if he gets in trouble he won't have to whisper, "HELP! HELP!") When we drove for miles through fields of cultivated sunflowers that stretched to the horizon in both directions with each flower exactly tracking the sun, we exchanged a smile. When Paul needed to pee or wanted coffee, he'd point at a truck stop up the road and nod. It was sort of like going for a long ride with a cat.

On our first morning we met Keith for breakfast at a café in Hill City and then followed him down paved and then dirt roads to a stream he liked. It was medium-size, meandering across a wide, flat valley with gravel bars, cut banks, and deep corner pools. The sight of this cold water seemed incongruous in these dry, rolling, pine-forested hills that looked black in the distance to pioneers.

I flushed grasshoppers ahead of me on the walk down to the water, so I naturally tied on a size 12 Dave's Hopper and fished it through three or four pools. Nothing. The hopper should have worked, so I bore down harder, trying for flawless dead drifts, and then tried snaking my hopper up against darkly undercut banks with little struggling upstream twitches I thought no trout could resist. Then I added a weighted dropper and broke it off on a snag on the first cast. The snag turned out to be an old roughly milled beam with corroded ironwork left over from a hundred-year-old mining operation.

An hour and a half later I still hadn't had a touch and was just going through the motions when a good-size brown trout nailed my hopper. It was so startling I only hooked him because he hooked himself and I managed not to drop the rod.

Paul had similar news: nothing for the longest time, then he'd found a small pod of rising trout in a corner pool and by casting, resting the water, and changing flies, he'd managed to get two foot-long brook trout.

Keith didn't offer a report, which could mean he'd landed a dozen trout, or none, or that as the perfect host he hadn't even fished.

On the walk back to our trucks we agreed that the day was too sunny and hot for the fish to be very active. In South Dakota, as in much of the mountain West, climate change has caused the seasons to slide forward by six weeks in recent decades, so that early September is now more like mid-July. Some of us fishermen haven't gotten used to that yet and I think the same goes for the trout.

Keith had to work that afternoon, but before he left he led us around more back roads to point out more creeks, getting us a little lost in the process. He'd drive for a while, and then stop so I could pull up beside him, blocking both lanes while we talked through our open windows.

After Keith left, Paul and I decided that what we needed was shade, so we picked a narrow creek that flowed out of the trees above a reservoir. It seemed fishless in the sunny stretches, but as soon as we got into the deep shade of the woods, trout would flash out from under the grassy banks to grab our hoppers, and in one bend pool with a current seam hugging the outside bank I landed a brown, a brook trout, and a rainbow on only twice that many casts. A South Dakota grand slam.

When I looked up from releasing the rainbow I realized I was in the manicured front yard of a cabin with a shiny new SUV parked in the driveway—clearly private land. My first instinct was to fade back into the trees before I was spotted, but the rule here, as it is in Montana, is that you can fish through any private property as long as you stay in the streambed. Keith said it took him years to get used to that and I understood what he meant. If a landowner saw you fishing in a place like this in Colorado, he'd call his lawyer; in Wyoming he might open fire, but in the Black Hills he'll just wave. The reception might be different if there were more fishermen around, but as it is only you, you just seem rustically harmless, especially when they can't see your pickup with its out-of-state plates.

That night Paul announced, in this gravelly, Don Corleone voice, that it was his birthday and he wanted pizza, so we asked around and got directions to a biker bar outside of Hill City that was reputed to have the best pizza in the county. We ordered a large with everything and the bartender said, "It's gonna take a while. All my summer help went back to college, so it's just me."

In fact the whole town had this same aspect of a place that's still open for business, but gradually winding down at the end of a long tourist season, with most of the part-time help and many of the tourists having fled back to their real lives. All that remained were weary locals, a handful of bikers left over from the Sturgis rally, and retirees in Winnebagos. Even the little 1950s vintage tourist cabin we'd rented came at a cheap, off-season rate. As for the bar, there were a few hogs in the gravel parking lot and Steppenwolf on the jukebox, but many of the bikers who'd been convincingly menacing back in the 1960s and '70s are now grandparents on Social Security who go to bed at nine o'clock, so the likelihood of mayhem seemed remote and the pizza was excellent.

The next day we tried one of the larger streams in the region where it flows out of the hills around Silver City. We parked at a gate where ours was the only vehicle in the pullout and walked up a gravel road that became a two-track and then tapered off into a foot trail along the water. This stream was said to be flowing high for September because of an unusually wet summer, but even then it would have been just barely big enough to thread a canoe down and you'd still have to walk the boat through the riffles.

The stream flowed through a ravine almost deep and narrow enough to be called a canyon, with the slopes forested in ponderosa pine and the stream banks overgrown with the kind of dense,

71

head-high brush that grabs your legs, tangles your fly rod, and plucks off your hat. One of the drawbacks to a shortage of fishermen is that there are no trails beaten down to the good pools, even though you could wish there were.

I blew what would have been my best South Dakota trout here. I'd made a down- and across-stream cast toward a logjam that blocked half of a bend pool: the kind of place where a big trout will wait out the middle of a hot day with the option of grabbing the odd grasshopper that drifts too close. The cast was good, but I'd misjudged the conflicting currents and the fly started to drag while it was still a few feet from the logs. So I threw an upstream mend that scooted the fly forward a few inches just as a brown trout no less than 18 inches long rolled at it and missed. It was the kind of accident of timing that defines a life in fishing and that you'd think you'd eventually get used to.

Later we got wind of a stream near Deadwood that had once been stocked with tiger trout and might still have some. A tiger trout is a cross between a brook trout and a brown, named for its distinctive tiger-like stripes. This hybrid can occur in nature, like a splake or a cuttbow, but it's rare. Most tiger trout are engineered in hatcheries by the kind of biologists who splice jellyfish genes into house cats to make kittens that glow in the dark. No telling why.

The streams in the Black Hills are kept cool by springs percolating through porous volcanic rock and they make for good trout habitat, but there were no trout here originally—the native fish ran to chubs, suckers, and sunfish—so fish culturists would have seen these creeks as a blank canvas, perfect for planting weird hybrids with no concern for their impact on indigenous trout. Anyway, neither of us had ever caught or even seen a tiger trout, so this stream became the kind of odd quest that sometimes fills the vacuum of an aimless fishing trip.

I got in at the bottom of a pool lying in the shade of a cliff and began casting my hopper to the tail-out just above the riffle. It was another cloudless day, already warm and heading toward hot, and this hundred yards of rock outcrop threw the only shade in sight. I could see Paul ahead of me casting to a pool at the upstream end of the cliff and vowed to fish my water as slowly as he fished his.

Paul is from Michigan, and like the other fishermen I know from that state, he's so persistent he can spend an hour on the same pool I'd breeze through in fifteen minutes with my typically western take-it-or-leave-it attitude. This is a regional trait they all share; it's as distinctive as the habit of holding up their hand with the fingers together and the thumb extended to make the mitten shape of the state and then pointing to where they're from. If I were keeping score I'd say that in the long run my Michigan friends and I usually come out about even in terms of fish caught, but they get theirs in a third less water than I do, so under oath I might be forced to admit that they're better fishermen.

I got three trout on the hopper in that pool, then, fighting off the urge to move on, I added a small Pheasant Tail dropper, fished through it again, and got another. After a ten-minute rest I switched to an Elk Hair caddis and got another trout, then added a soft hackle dropper to that and got two more. After another, longer rest I fished through again with the same hopper I'd started with and got one more fish right up at the head of the pool. It was the biggest one: a brown about 14 inches long that I'd never have seen if I'd fished on through on the first pass. I don't know how long I spent on this spot, but it was long enough for the shadow of the cliff to sidle halfway across the pool. I vowed to slow down my fishing pace from here on out.

From there we fished around a bend and worked up through two more pools and on into a long stretch of riffles punctuated by narrow slicks, all in full, hot sun. We got a few more fish, but they were

mostly small—nothing like the nice ones from the shady cliff pools—
and they were the usual mix of brookies, browns, and rainbows. We
never saw a tiger trout, but there's an odd footnote. A month later
I caught one while fishing the olive hatch on the Frying Pan River
back in Colorado. It didn't register at first, but there was nothing
else it could have been with those paisley stripes on its flanks and a
blush of tigerish orange on the belly. In forty years of fishing the Pan,
no one I know had ever seen or even heard of a tiger trout in that
river, or anywhere else in Colorado for that matter. When the guys at
the fly shop in town saw a photo of it, all they could say was "Huh?"
It was a head-scratcher.

Paul was back in Michigan by then and I sent him the photo. I
said my best guess was that it was an errant fish stocked by a landowner or that somehow got into a load of hatchery rainbows by mistake, but that it's possible it was a rare natural cross. After all, there
are brown trout in the Pan and although brook trout aren't as common as they once were, they do still turn up now and then. Maybe
one autumn a brown trout with eclectic tastes took a shine to one of
those painted ladies from back east.

He wrote back that it was "the fulfillment of incipient karma,"
period. Even before his voice became barely audible, Paul was a
man of few words.

8.

LARGE, DARK, AND WULFFISH

By mid-afternoon the temperature had reached 103 degrees and my writer friend Scott Sadil and I were holed up on the shady side of the Black Bear Lodge overlooking the Columbia River. We'd escaped the direct sun, but the heat was like a wool blanket that you couldn't throw off and we sat there feeling unpleasantly sedated, with the ice in our drinks long since melted. There'd been some others out there with us earlier, including my fishing partner, Vince, but by then they'd all drifted away. People sometimes like to eavesdrop when writers sit down to talk—maybe hoping to learn something about the creative process—but after half an hour of whining about money and the character assassinations of editors, they tend to wander off.

We were all just killing time until the fishing started. That wouldn't happen until around six o'clock, but by a quarter to five Vince and I would be motoring upriver with our guide to get a jump on it and, not incidentally, for the cool breeze of the ride. We'd assembled here in early July to fish the nighttime Black Drake hatch and were now mimicking these mayflies' behavior by waiting out the lethal heat of the days and stirring only when the sun went off the water.

We knew that on the way upriver that evening we'd pass Scott and his friend Steve Bird at their usual spot on a long backwater. Steve is a guide, writer, blogger, and fly tier who's known hereabouts as the local fly-fishing guru—a "neo-classicist" by his own admission, with a weakness for soft-hackled wet flies, 1950s-vintage fiberglass rods, and nonmotorized fishing boats. This backwater was once known as Big Eddy because of its size, but has since been renamed Steve's Eddy by the guides, who've declared it off-limits out of respect.

This was the American stretch of the Columbia, so-called because it's where the river enters the United States in the far northeastern corner of Washington State. The border with Canada here is marked by nothing more than a cable across the river that doesn't seem to be fortified or even guarded, although I was told that if you ducked under that cable you'd quickly get a different impression.

I'd seen the Columbia at its full size closer to Puget Sound, and although it's somewhat smaller this far upriver, it's already drained the entire Southern Rocky Mountain Trench in British Columbia—flowing north for a while, then doglegging south, collecting tributaries—so by the time it crosses the border the river's normal midsummer flow of 100,000 cubic feet of water per second already makes it seem vast and intimidating.

This Black Drake hatch was a new one on me. I'd chased plenty of other drake hatches and once, for several late nights running, the even larger Hexagenia mayflies in northern Wisconsin. The prevailing myth among fly-fishers is that the big mayflies drive trout insane, and although "insane" might be overstating it a little, it *is* true that these large bugs often bring the biggest trout to the surface, where you can fish for them with dry flies. There are too many variables to ever make it a sure thing, but over the years the possibility alone has cost me a fortune in gas money and plane tickets with no end in sight.

On our first night out with our guide, C.J., Vince and I got the new clients' orientation in the style of fishing known locally as "free-drifting." C.J. said there'd be occasional scum-suckers sipping spent caddis in the quieter water along the banks, but that we'd ignore those in favor of the real action to Drakes out in midriver. Once the rise got started, C.J. would find a current line he liked the looks of, cock the boat sideways to the flow, and hold the angle steady with the oars as we drifted straight downstream at current speed, which always turned out to be faster than it looked.

The current in midriver boiled up in response to the jumbled boulders on the bottom, the water rolling over on itself and wagging every which way like the tails of enormous wet dogs. As we drifted along we'd cast downstream to slicks that would form, swirl down with the current for a few yards, and then dissolve, only to be replaced by fresh ones. It was in the foamy leading edges of these slicks that the big duns would collect and the trout would rise.

This wasn't how Vince and I would have done it, and in fact it seemed overly aggressive and even wasteful to drift straight down to, and right over, multiple rising trout—one all-or-nothing cast and the whole pod was blown—but telling your guide he's doing it wrong on the first night out is the kind of advanced move that's best left to experts.

This was fast-paced fishing and the trick was to make short, accurate casts and drifts to avoid drag. You'd think trout in this maelstrom of moving water and failing light would forgive a fly that skated a little, but no such luck. The second your fly did the least little thing that wasn't dictated entirely by the current, you might as well recast it to another slick because the jig was up.

We were after the big redband trout that are native to the Columbia drainage. It's probably fair to think of these fish as a subspecies of rainbow, but many fisheries biologists consider them to be distinct, although in the grand scheme of things that may boil down to an opinion. I once fished with a doctoral candidate in fisheries biology who explained that among taxonomists there's an innate tension between the lumpers and the splitters. A lumper would say that there's only the one species called rainbow trout that exhibit some regional variations, while a splitter would say that virtually every watershed is home to its own separate race of fish. My friend was a confirmed lumper himself and left the impression that he thought splitters tended toward hysteria. But my sympathies lie with the splitters for the simple reason that if they're right, then there are even more kinds of fish in the world than I thought.

To the scientifically untrained eye of a fisherman, a redband has a more profuse spotting pattern than a coastal rainbow and the lateral line stripe is less crimson and more the deep red color of wet brick. These are gorgeous fish; not the sickly, mass-produced versions of rainbow trout that have been raised in hatcheries and stocked all over the West for more than a century, but a strain of ancestral trout rightfully famous for their beauty, size, and fight. You don't have to catch many of them before you start wondering how fish culturists managed to turn such fine wild trout into generic lunch meat.

There must have been some small fish somewhere, but one reason to work the fast water is that that's where the big boys go to feed. These were heavy, muscular trout between 18 and 24 inches long and sometimes much larger. It seemed like every night back at camp someone had a story about setting up on a fish that bored off unstoppably until the weight of the current against all that line and backing either broke off the fly or straightened the hook. Some couldn't help guessing at the size of those trout, while others just shrugged. In each case it had seemed hopeless almost from the beginning, but no fisherman believes it's ever *completely* hopeless, so they wondered if they'd screwed it up. You could see that in their faces: something akin to embarrassment at blowing the big chance, along with the knowledge that a big lost fish can haunt you until you redeem yourself on this or some future river by landing a pig against the odds.

Night fishing is always a moving target. At first it's just a pleasant early evening with the day's heat finally beginning to lift and the sunlight going off the water, retreating up the east bank until just the crowns of the pines are lit like the flames at the tips of a forest of matches. That's when the first Drake duns appeared in scattered ones and twos. As mayflies go, they were on the big side; about a hook size 8 or 10 with dark reddish-brown bodies and slate-colored wings, or "large, dark, and Wulffish," as I'd once heard them described. The first few floated along until their wings dried and they could fly off without drawing any interest from the trout, but there was the sense that something was about to happen and we imagined that the nymphs migrating up from the riverbed were already getting picked off by large trout.

By the time we spotted the first rises the surface of the river had already turned silver, but there was still enough light to see a low-floating Victory Drake as long as you didn't take your eyes off it and lose it in the confusion of currents. It took time to play and land each fish we hooked because of their size and strength as well as the heavy current that gave them the mechanical advantage. We were fishing short casts, but most of our trout took us well into the backing before C.J. could row us into quieter water where we could play them to the net.

Every time I looked back at the river after a fish was released I was surprised and a little panicked by how much darker it had gotten. A friend once said he prefers evening fishing because morning fishing peters out as time passes, while evening fishing only gets better. That's true, but sooner than you'd like evening becomes night, your diurnal nature betrays you, and where only a few minutes ago you were a reasonably competent fly caster, you're now fumbling for the light switch in a strange hotel room, defeated by darkness.

As soon as I started losing sight of my Victory Drake on every other cast, I switched to one of the big parachute Wulffs I'd tied with oversize black calf tail wings that were easier to see. But even then I found myself squinting, squatting, and cocking my head left and right to get my fly in whatever pewter-colored night shine was left on the surface. By then each fish we got had to be landed and unhooked by the light of our headlamps, and once we'd turn the lights off it would take valuable minutes for our eyes to readjust enough to start casting again. Eventually they didn't readjust no matter how long we waited because it was just too damned dark. That's when we reeled in our flies, C.J. rigged the legally required running lights (red for port, green for starboard), and we motored back toward camp.

It was going on midnight; the shoreline was only a little blacker than the water and the sky was full of stars. Our big johnboat was fitted with a 60-horse outboard and we were flying downriver faster than I'd have gone in the dark. I could tell the Drakes were still hatching because they kept hitting me in the face, but by then it was impossible to see a dry fly and you couldn't fish by sound because the river was too loud to hear the rises. It would still have been possible to swing a big wet fly downstream on a tight line so you could feel the takes, but it was late and Vince and I had been into our backing more times in the last five hours than in the whole previous season, so we were happy enough to call it a night and it was somehow comforting to know that this would all go on without us for a few more hours.

By the third night I'd begun to learn the landmarks, so that on the trip back downriver I recognized the dark shapes of the forested island, the big midriver boulder, and the long, sweeping riffle known as Lower Magic. I was waiting for the scattered lights of the little town of Northport to appear on river left when I saw flashes in the sky above the water, followed after an interval by the dull thumps of distant fireworks, and remembered it was the Fourth of July. Northport is one of those remote western towns with less than three hundred souls who can't afford to patch the potholes on Main Street, but who can still pony up thousands every year for Chinese-made patriotic ordnance.

So we motored through town in a shower of hot multicolored sparks and after we passed under the hulking shape of the bridge C.J. handed out Roman candles with labels promising "sparkling balls with reports." As he lit these up, he advised us to "point them away from the boat," which contained, among other things, a five-gallon can of gasoline. And that's how we pulled into camp: shooting off sparkling balls with reports to scattered applause from the porch of the lodge.

That night I was the one with a story to tell. Dark as it had been, I was sure I'd seen my fly go down in a boil. But when I set up I felt nothing but dead weight moving at current speed and thought I'd snagged a drifting log—the kind of deadhead you hope the boat doesn't hit when you're flying along at top speed. But then it started moving across the current, slowly at first, then accelerating steadily toward the distant far bank while my line and backing bellied out downstream. I put a deep bend in the rod and got two fingers inside the reel spool to put the brakes on my departing backing, but the fish didn't even slow down. It seemed hopeless almost from the beginning.

I can't say exactly when it happened, but I gradually came to realize that I was no longer attached to the fish—it had been lost not with a bang, but a whimper—and when I reeled in the entire fly line and nearly a hundred yards of backing I found that my knot had held, but the hook was bent open. I'd had plenty of time to see this coming, but I still couldn't believe it. The redbands here occasionally exceed 20 pounds, so when someone at the lodge asked how big I thought the fish was, I said, a little petulantly, that I didn't know and didn't even *want* to know.

Steve Bird had invited Vince and me to fish with him the next night, so we snagged a ride to his place in the afternoon and hung out there, waiting for evening to come on. It was still as hot as the doorknob to hell and we'd been dreading having to kill another hundred-plus-degree day at the lodge. It hadn't been so bad at first, but after days of boredom, idleness, and discomfort, the veneer of carefree sport had begun to peel back at the edges and the normal chafing among the personnel was threatening to harden into grudges. The little air-conditioning unit at the lodge ground away valiantly, but couldn't put a dent in the heat, no one's jokes were funny anymore, and I lost interest in the mystery novel I was reading when I stopped caring who the killer was. Vince and I weren't exactly at the end of our rope, but we *were* feeling the need for new company and a fresh patch of shade to swelter in.

Steve and his wife, Doris, live in a snug, efficient frame house on the edge of the pine woods, close to the river, but safely above the high-water line. There are two outhouses in back, a large vegetable

one morning and it was over." But in this case there
e regret that accompanies questions of faithfulness.
spot doesn't care if you fish it anymore or not. In fact,
e, it would probably just as soon you didn't.
dozen ponds here spread out over some two hun-
gravel quarries that were abandoned early in the last
ntually filled with groundwater and went wild. This
en a light-industrial wasteland once, but when I first
n the early 1970s it was fully grown up in groves of
d locust with the stark edges of the ponds softened
nes, and the two-track dirt access roads devolved into
could still tell that these weren't naturally formed
hen you had to look twice.

he usual hodgepodge of bluegills, catfish, largemouth
Some people claimed that these fish first arrived ac-
gs stuck to the legs of herons, but a fisheries biologist
at was unlikely. The insects, frogs, and turtles would
pped, or walked from nearby wetlands, but the fish
ave been stocked. The bird leg theory made intuitive
because these ponds had the feel of a place that had
abandoned, and forgotten, and had since gone wild
own. It was hard not to imagine biology itself single-
ming the landscape.

irly new to Colorado then, one of thousands of young
d decided we didn't want to live at arm's length from
oved as we'd seen others do. (My father loved to fish
he had the time, but he almost never had the time.)
more specific than that. We've been characterized—
hose who weren't there—as true believers in a social
volution, but for many of us it was simply that we

garden behind a fence tall and sturdy enough to keep out deer and elk, and two big, lazy cats that lounged in the shade like hothouse orchids. Scott's tent was back in the trees a discreet distance from the house, pitched over a natural mattress of pine duff.

When the time came we launched Steve's raft on the eddy, where we stayed in the soft water and cast out to the main current. Steve kept us more or less motionless with the occasional dip of an oar while Vince and I worked the moving windows of the slicks that passed by, getting decent drifts by casting down and across with steep upstream mends. Instead of making one all-or-nothing cast and then moving on as we'd been doing, we were able to work pods of big trout until we finally put them down by either catching one or dragging a cast, and then we'd quietly ease along to the next pod of risers. The eddy was nearly half a mile long, so when we reached the bottom we'd simply row back to the top, where the trout had been rested for almost an hour, and start again. Fished in this stealthy, unhurried way, that one small reach of river was all anyone could ask for and it seemed more like recognizable fly-fishing, which I've always thought should be less like a mugging than a con game.

I asked Steve why he thought the guides at the lodge fished so aggressively and needlessly burned up so much water. He said it was because that's how the owner wanted it done and went on to characterize the way some people fish as if he were describing the plumage of an unfamiliar bird, adding something to the effect that it's a free country and people can fish however they want.

It was just about full dark when I got a hideous tangle of fly line around my rod tip with a disastrous cast. I'd just started trying to pick this mess apart by the light of my headlamp when Steve tapped me on the shoulder and handed me an old Heddon fiberglass rod fitted with a Pflueger Medalist reel, already strung up with a dark brown soft-hackled wet fly. And that's what I used to catch my last redband of the night, a hefty, broad-shouldered fish that ran and cartwheeled somewhere out in the darkness. My first fly reel had been a Pflueger and I'd forgotten that these old American-made reels purr instead of scream when a fish takes line.

The next night Vince and I asked C.J. if he'd be willing to fish the same way. Without a word—but possibly the hint of a sly smile—he rowed us into quiet water and positioned us so deftly that Vince said later, "I bet that's how he fishes on his days off."

We were leaving the next morning and for once the timing seemed about right. We'd cleaned up on big trout and, now that we'd soon be flying back to the cooler high altitude of home in Colorado, waiting out those miserably hot, boring days began to look like a fair price of admission for epic night fishing, if not actually a noble sacrifice for sport. There'd be plenty of time to wonder if we'd ever want to do this again.

All in all, I was feeling pretty pleased with myself, so when we got back to the lodge that night I gave my last few parachute Black Drakes to a father and his teenage son who'd just arrived. There seemed to be a specific plan in the works with these two; probably just the usual attempt to engineer some good memories before life inevitably threw one or the other of them a curve. I resolved to just give them some flies that had worked without the usual territorial display that inevitably accompanies male success in sport, but when the moment came I couldn't resist just enough grandstanding to make me feel smug at the time and a little foolish later. Vanity does loosen its grip on us over time, but I guess it never completely lets go.

BLUEGILLS

These ponds are only half from the foothills and onto last time I'd been there. C able memories and settled cause pinning down an exa I couldn't put my finger or It had always been profou about it—but that was pr finally drift away. It's the sai their once-happy marriage

"I just woke up was none of th Your old sweet given the choic

There are dred acres: old century and ev would have be saw the place cottonwood an by cattail marsh foot trails. You ponds, but by t

There was bass, and carp. cidentally as eg I asked said th have flown, ho would have to sense, though, been used up, entirely on its handedly reclai

I was still fa drop-outs who' the things we l and went when I can't be much sometimes by and political re

knew what we *didn't* want, but were still unclear about the alternative. Remember, the term was "dropping out," not "signing on."

I'd fallen hard for everything about the Rocky Mountains from day one—with trout and the places they lived at the top of the list—and I'd taken up fly-fishing. I enjoyed its fussy Old World pretensions, but although I understood the practical virtue of that new idea known as catch-and-release fishing, I also ate a lot of trout. If nothing else, they were free, and when you worked cheap and had time on your hands, free was good. Still, it was trout and fried potatoes, trout and rice, or trout and beans until the occasional cheeseburger began to taste like beef Wellington.

If nothing else, these warm water ponds varied the menu. I'd grown up eating bluegills, I liked them, and, more to the point, I knew how to catch and cook them. Trout were a real challenge to me then (still are) and catching them wasn't a foregone conclusion, but under the right conditions catching bluegills was like picking raspberries; all you had to know was where they were and when they were ripe.

The trick was to find them spawning, which they do in the spring when the water temperature reaches about 67 degrees and stays there for a while. It doesn't matter if the weather goes sideways and the water cools off again; they'll simply abandon the beds and come back later, and even when they spawn successfully in the spring they'll sometimes do it all over again for good measure in early summer. These horny, persistent fish seem ready at a moment's notice like the male leads in porn films and that was the justification for keeping spawners. It was said that bluegills reproduced so prolifically that you could take as many as you wanted without doing any harm. Like all fish management philosophies of the "Aw hell, it don't hurt nothin'" variety, it was true only up to a point.

It was a simple matter of walking around the ponds starting in mid-April looking for the colonies of shallow, saucer-sized spawning beds that bluegills excavate in no more than a few feet of water. Sometimes they were hard to pick out against a dark bottom and other times they were as obvious as fresh elephant tracks, but once you knew where they were you could walk right to them the way you'd go straight to the fish counter in a grocery store. I was using a fly rod by then, but these fish would eat any nymph or wet fly in a size 14 as readily as they'd eaten pieces of worm on small bait hooks when I was six years old.

There were never many people at these ponds, just the odd bird watcher and a handful of blue-collar bass fishermen who I rarely talked to. They thought I was a hippie, I thought they were rednecks, and that was pretty much the end of it. The most that usually passed between us was the kind of meaningful nod that acknowledges a truce without relinquishing the underlying grudge. But it turned out that we weren't as different as we thought and a process of mutual assimilation had already begun. Before long, ponytails started to outnumber crew cuts on some landscaping and construction sites and the proximity of work led to the usual cultural exchange so that in some cowboy roadhouses Commander Cody and the Lost Planet Airmen appeared next to Waylon Jennings on the jukeboxes. Not many years later William Kitteridge would write, "Things are looking up. Rednecks take drugs; hippies take jobs."

In the years after the fall of Saigon I'd sometimes see Vietnamese refugee families fishing the ponds. They used cane poles and bait and, judging by the galvanized buckets they filled with fish, they knew what they were doing. There might be three generations together, with the mama-sans in "coolie" hats and the grandkids in baseball caps and Snoopy T-shirts shyly acting as interpreters. I never learned their stories; mostly we just complimented each other's catch in passing and there was some awkward bowing on my part in response to their elaborate politeness.

The closest I ever came to a run-in with one of the rednecks was when a guy told me my "gook friends" oughta be arrested for keeping too many fish and I informed him that with a daily bag limit of twenty bluegills, that family of five could legally bring home a hundred of them if they wanted to. The guy got pretty steamed, but in hindsight, I don't think he was really all that mad. I think he just saw me as ridiculous with my long hair and beard, prissy little fly rod, and a stringer of what he'd have considered kids' fish. He probably just thought I was giving the sport a bad name.

But who could resist bluegills with their handsome coloring, their sleepy brown eyes, and their adorable willingness when spawning to eat anything they could get their mouths around? And they're so beautifully adapted to avoid being eaten themselves. Their frying-pan-on-end shape makes even small ones awkward to swallow and their sharp, spiny dorsal fins enhance the effect. One of the first things I learned as a kid was how to comb down a bluegill's fin with my thumb so I could hold it without getting stuck.

In ideal conditions bluegills can weigh as much as a couple of pounds, but they usually aren't that large. The rule I was taught growing up was that a bluegill that completely covered your hand was a keeper—and I don't have particularly large hands. A fish that size using its flat sides to plane against the pull of the line puts a satisfying bend in a light fly rod, or as Al McClane once wrote in his laconic way, a bluegill "is not spectacular, but it resists vigorously."

A stringer of ten hand-size bluegills (half a limit) would give you a dinner of twenty succulent miniature fillets that resembled fish sticks, but tasted better. They were best when lightly beer-battered and deep-fried in Crisco, although out here in the wild Southwest, bluegill tacos were also a possibility. At the time I had it in mind to beat the system by living off the land, although to be honest the fish I brought home didn't cut all that significantly into the grocery bill. But what they *did* do was train me in the kind of subversively creative thinking that kept the system at arm's length. That would come in handy later when I became a writer and continued to live by my wits into middle age and beyond.

And there was something comforting about those ponds. The snowcapped Continental Divide on the western horizon and the occasional prickly pear cactus were constant reminders that I was on the high plains of Colorado—an exotic location for a kid from the heartland—but otherwise the green, lush funk of the place was as distinctly midwestern as any of the farm ponds I'd fished as a kid. I didn't feel at all homesick and wouldn't have admitted it if I did. I was just experiencing the same impulse that makes an American visiting Moscow want to stop at a McDonald's.

Once the spawn ended it became less like berry picking and more like real fishing. The bluegills scattered out in the ponds, the little ones sticking to the shallows, the bigger ones holding deeper where they'd split the difference between feeding and hugging sunken structures for protection. They'd have spawned roughly according to size, which was real handy, but later they'd congregate for less obvious reasons that often had to be worked out on the spot: water depth, temperature, cover, food, shade, and so on—the usual puzzle. Getting enough for dinner took more time, which meant more time spent fishing, which wasn't all bad.

I especially liked casting small poppers in the evenings after work and as an aspiring purist I decided to make my own. My best had pencil-thin sanded cork bodies, feather tails, and rubber legs. The paint jobs were chartreuse overall with a scale pattern on the back made with contrasting spray paint and a piece of old aquarium net as a stencil, plus the usual black-on-white painted eyes. I tried other colors, but as the bass fishermen say, "You can't lose with chartreuse." Commercial poppers are usually dipped in paint, which is efficient in terms of mass production, but fouls the eyes of the hooks. I told anyone who'd listen that you can always spot a hand-painted popper because the eye is clean.

Some ponds were naturally better than others and I had my favorites. The best was way back in the southwest corner, a twenty-minute walk and as far from the parking lot as you could get. The east end of that pond was uniformly deep and featureless, but on the west side the bottom sloped gradually and there were channels surrounded by grassy hummocks of old spoil where the workers who dug the quarries had lost the gravel seam and had dug test trenches trying to pick it up again.

This pond regularly had the biggest bluegills and the most extensive spawning areas, and it was a little dicey to get around in the boggy cattail marsh on the west end, where the fishing was best, so I usually had it to myself. Most years there was an active osprey nest just east of the pond and one of the adults was often perched in a nearby cottonwood looking as regal as the finial on a flagpole. The bird would glare at me while I fished as if it begrudged me every bluegill I put on a stringer.

For a while my fly rod was the only one I ever saw on the ponds, but later two fly-fishing friends sometimes came along, including one who was living with me while he sorted things out long-distance with his wife. These guys were both from the Midwest themselves and remembered bluegills fondly, but they were unusual. At the time most fly fishermen—at least the fancy ones—were trout specialists who looked down their noses at lesser fish and, by implication, lesser fishermen. Some of those guys started calling me "Grits." It wasn't meant to be a flattering nickname.

I did spend some time out there fishing for the bass. Now and then I'd pick up a small one while fishing poppers for bluegills and I assumed there'd be bigger ones somewhere. After all, the rednecks were bass guys and there's always the suspicion that other fishermen know something you don't. This was also about the time that Dave Whitlock was repopularizing fly-fishing for bass—and coincidentally selling the bejesus out of his beautifully tied deer hair bass bugs—so it was in the air. I made some hair bugs of my own that worked well enough, although they took forever to construct and fell far short of the standard of craftsmanship set by Whitlock.

I did my best by casting from a float tube into the stickiest cover I could find, fishing at dusk and on past dark on summer evenings. The county had posted a sign saying that the ponds were closed from dusk till dawn, but the cops would only swing by on slow nights and even then they'd rarely show up before midnight. They were looking for beer-drinking or pot-smoking teenagers and didn't really care about fishermen, but they'd ticket your car anyway, so I tried to be off the water by eleven.

These didn't turn out to be great bass ponds. Every now and then I'd hang one that approached 15 inches long and sometimes—rarely—I'd get one a little bigger. I'd grown up in bass country and understood that these were just barely keepers, but I'd occasionally invite one home for dinner anyway.

Then a friend and I discovered some lakes in the Nebraska Sandhills that had much larger bass and, coincidentally, bluegills that could weigh a pound or more. We also fished some bass tanks in South Texas where a local fisherman asked us to "keep some 'a them little five-pounders for supper" and not long after that I started going to northern Wisconsin to float placid rivers for smallmouth bass. By then I'd capitulated and was buying Whitlock Swimming Frogs in two sizes and colors.

And of course there were always trout, which took up more and more of my fishing time until they became the gold standard. There were the trout close to home and those farther away in the northern Rockies and on into Canada, where I assumed they'd be bigger and sometimes they were, not to mention sexier fish like steelhead and Atlantic and Pacific salmon that lived even farther away. By then I'd become just solvent enough to have some disposable income and I learned that no travel agent would talk me out of disposing of it thinking the fishing was better somewhere else.

It turned out that the real big fish in these ponds were the carp. I'd been seeing them all along, but never paid any attention until some midwesterners began promoting them as a fly rod fish. They called them "backyard bonefish" and said they were most people's only chance to fish within an hour's drive of home and hook a 10-pounder that would take them into the backing.

I didn't have a high opinion of carp—we'd always considered them to be trash fish—so I assumed they couldn't be all that hard to catch, but they turned out to be pickier and warier than brown trout. I had to bear down hard and even then it took more afternoons of stalking, casting, and fly changing than I care to admit before I hooked one that did, in fact, weigh around 10 pounds and took me right into the backing on its first run. I stayed with it long enough to learn the ropes a little and eventually catch an 18-pounder that took fifteen minutes to land. It was a thrilling fight and a magnificent fish, but it was still just a carp, at which point the novelty started to wear off. And that was it for me and the ponds. I just woke up one morning and it was over.

Going back out there, however many years later, I half-expected everything to look smaller—like when you return to the house where you were born when you're no longer three feet tall—but everything was the same. The last time I'd been there they'd already gentrified the place with a fancy two-hole outhouse and a handicapped fishing pier, which, like so many of those things, was situated in the perfect location to build a pier, but not such a great place to fish. And they'd already installed the big sign listing all the things you shouldn't do, including keep a bass less than 15 inches long and fish bait in any of the ponds except the first two.

At the time those rules hadn't made an impression on some of the rednecks who continued to keep 9- and 10-inch bass and fish bait in the back ponds, but then there have always been three kinds of fishermen: those who read and obey the rules, those who read them so they'll know what to hide, and those who ignore the rules entirely out of a pioneer's sense of entitlement. My father was scrupulous about regulations, as I am now, but at a tender age my black sheep uncle showed me the dark side in detail, so you could say I'm able to be objective about this.

I didn't go to the ponds that day as a conscious act of nostalgia, but because I had a spring afternoon to kill, couldn't remember the last time I'd caught a bluegill, and just got a wild hair. It took five minutes to pack a 9-foot fly rod, a spool of tippet, and a box with weighted nymphs and cork poppers. And on the way out to the truck I grabbed my old chain stringer in case I found a pod of big bluegills. I hadn't carried that stringer in years, but I remembered right where it was: hanging on a nail inside the garage door, covered with dust like an antique waiting to be rediscovered.

10.

SHAKEDOWN CRUISE

It was a frigid morning at State Bridge on the upper Colorado River, with thick clouds piled up against the west slope of the Rockies and an icy fog over the water, sealing in the cold night air like a lid. This was the last week in October, but everything about the day felt like January. The big paved parking lot at the put-in had enough room for forty trucks and trailers, but we were the only ones there. That meant we'd have this whole stretch of river to ourselves, but may also have meant we were the only ones dumb enough to want it. But never mind. Vince had been repairing and refinishing his wooden drift boat for most of the summer and was desperate to get it in the water at least once this season. So we wadered up, pulled the cover off the boat, left the use fee in the drop box and cash and keys in the truck for the shuttle driver, and launched on an empty river.

This boat was built by Ray's River Dories in Portland, Oregon, in 1990, and although I'd never been in it before, I'd seen it around for years. At first it was owned by a friend who, like most fishermen with jobs, families, and mortgages, used the boat as often as he could, but not as often as he'd have liked. Mostly it sat in the driveway while he was off running his landscaping business, lending an air of postponed adventure to a suburban neighborhood in Boulder, Colorado.

I'd always liked the looks of it. It's a well-made and handsome Rogue River–style drift boat, but it's not ostentatious in the way of those wooden craft that are intended to come off more like pieces of Chippendale furniture than fishing boats. This one was clearly built for use and looked like it had had plenty. By the time I first saw it, it already had the used but far from used-up look of an old and handy tool.

And it was nicely put together. The sides, seats, and decks are made of Sapele African mahogany; the gunnels, chines, seats, and stem post are Honduran mahogany; and the boat frames and seats are straight-grained Douglas fir. The wood inside is finished with oil, and outside it's painted a shade of green that reminds me of a John Deere tractor with a spar-varnished natural wood rub rail at the waterline. As drift boats go, it's on the small side: 14 feet, 10 inches stem to stern (16 feet measured around the gunnels) with a 74-inch beam tapering to a bottom width of 48 inches. Viewed side-on, its lines are reminiscent of a floating leaf.

Vince eventually ended up owning it through a roundabout series of transactions. First he bought it from the landscaper for the kind of price he tends to get on things like this, which is more than fair, but somewhere short of outright theft. Then, just when I'd gotten used to seeing it parked in his driveway, he sold it for a profit without ever putting it in the water. And then, two years later, it reappeared; bought back at a bargain price as a fixer-upper because by then it needed work that the owner hadn't gotten around to doing. He must have finally gotten tired of looking at it—or maybe of *it* seeming to look at *him* accusingly—and he just let it go. It was beginning to look like Vince was somehow meant to own this boat.

But it really did need work. By this time the casting brace and fly line deck were both cracked (no telling how that happened), the bottom was splintered near the stern where the anchor had either been dropped unceremoniously or left to bounce around on a bumpy road, and the routine cleaning, sanding, and refinishing were so long overdue that spots of ominous black mold had appeared on the deck. This is why wooden boats aren't for everyone: If you put in the time and effort to take care of them they'll last for a hundred years, but if you treat them like they're unbreakable or blow off the maintenance, they'll begin to delaminate.

Vince was just the guy to own a boat in this condition. He not only enjoys this kind of work, but he has the tools and the required woodworking skill as well as the kind of untroubled ego that lets him sniff out people who know more than he does for advice and then to take it. For instance, when he called the builder to ask about a replacement piece of mahogany for the fly deck, the man told him to just go to Home Depot and pick out a nice piece of birch plywood, which he did after sorting through dozens of sheets of the stuff to find the best one.

For months, every time I stopped at Vince's house, he'd take me to the garage to show me what he'd recently done to the boat, or explain what he was planning to do next. Vince is no stranger to boats, but this was his first wooden one and by then he was reeling off the arcane nomenclature—inside chine log, swivel block, stem cap, sheer rail—and he was getting pretty attached to the craft. It was a bigger job than he'd anticipated, but wood is warm, friendly stuff to work with and all that fitting, sanding, gluing, brushing, and rubbing on of oil is like stroking a large, docile animal: it engenders intimacy and affection and incidentally lowers blood pressure.

Naturally Vince took the oars that first day on the water. I automatically stood up in the bow with a streamer rod and stripped out some line, but sat back down when I saw we'd be putting the boat through its paces. Vince rowed across the river and then back the other way, he draw-stroked first left and then right, tracked quietly in the main current for a minute—chopping the oars lightly—then spun the boat in midriver and pulled smartly back upstream in a moderate current, the whole time wearing the discerning expression of a wine critic.

"It's nice," he said. "It handles nice; real light and responsive. In fact, it handles better than my old [fill in the blank with a well-known maker of fiberglass drift boats]."

Then he said, "Okay," and I stood back up and began working out line as we approached casting distance of the right bank.

This was the kind of gloomy day that can make for good fishing and we were on a stretch of river that's known to hold lots of trout, but not many of them were interested in my streamer that day. The ones that *were* interested were holding tight and wouldn't chase it more than two or three feet off the bank, so I was making long casts, a few short, quick strips, and then picking up a lot of line for the next throw. About the time it occurred to me that this would be easier if we were a little closer to the bank, the boat eased in a little closer to the bank as if I were controlling it telepathically. When you fish together long enough, this sort of thing happens so thoughtlessly that you don't have to ask and sometimes forget to say thanks.

The weather that day could have gone either way. Up on the pass on the drive over that morning the sky was clear blue and the sun on the snow was as blinding as a spotlight, so there was the thought that the clouds in the valley could burn off by early afternoon to produce one of those splendidly crisp, bright autumn days. But the two slopes of the Continental Divide can be like different planets, and instead the ceiling on the west side lowered and thickened through the day, the air stayed dank and cold, and by midmorning a stinging rain had begun—not quite sleet, but leaning in that direction and hinting that it could turn to snow by dusk.

By the time a train passed on the tracks that share this valley with the river—slowing to walking speed as it rounded a tight curve fifty feet from the water—we were bundled in every stitch of warm clothes we'd brought, topped off with rain gear, hats with ear flaps, and fingerless wool gloves. In the popular vision of drift boats as seen on calendars and in magazine ads, they're always out on sunny, windless days with snow-capped mountains in the middle distance and smiling fishermen in shirtsleeves, but rarely in cold, gray drizzle with the mountains buried in clouds. We must have looked like discouraged gnomes to the passengers who gazed at us as blankly as TV watchers from their warm train windows. We gazed back just as expressionlessly until one guy—possibly a fisherman—waved at us and we waved back. Once the train had passed, the river seemed even more vacant than it had before.

I took the oars after lunch and before we settled down to fishing I rowed around for a few minutes to get the feel of the boat. When I first rowed in current I made all the standard mistakes, digging the oars too deep, overcorrecting, and most of all not reading the water right or thinking far enough ahead. I hadn't yet learned to stop fighting the river and relax into it, so at the end of my first day of rowing I was exhausted. But eventually it became obvious that a drift boat is like a dry fly: if you put it in the right place upstream, it'll drift to the right place downstream on its own with only minor adjustments for speed and angle, which involves less muscle than forethought. A good oarsman is like a pool player who not only makes the shot at hand, but sets himself up for the *next* shot. Done right, it looks deceptively easy because most of the work is mental. I got some coaching along the way from guides and friends, but mostly I learned through the usual process of fucking up, remembering why, and vowing not to do it again. Which is to say, I'm not one of the great boatmen, but I manage.

At a bare minimum, you try to get down the river without hitting anything, but in the fullness of time bumps and scrapes are inevitable. This boat is equipped with a composite skid plate that makes scraping on shallow riffles less agonizing, and, like bamboo rods, wooden boats are tougher than you think, but it's still possible to ding the chines, crack the hull, or worse. It doesn't help that this is the kind of pretty boat that other fishermen will walk over and admire, sometimes asking if you're worried about putting it on the river. The answer is, "What else would I do with it?"

Still, floating a river can be a distracting business with scenery, wildlife, drifting dry flies, running conversations, and fish to net all competing for your limited attention, but current is inexorable and a surprisingly short lapse in concentration can put you too far into trouble to get out of gracefully. You'll see drift boats with the motto "Fear No Rock" stenciled on them, which I always thought must be meant ironically, since an oarsman who truly fears no rock will sooner or later end up wet with all his expensive gear on the bottom of the river.

And of course it's all in the service of the fisherman. The boat's angle, speed, and distance from the bank all depend on the cast and drift that have to be made as well as on the fisherman who has to make them. Under ideal conditions, you arrange things so that the best bank or seam passes right at your sport's comfortable casting range, but conditions are rarely ideal, so you work out how best to split the difference. Like anything else, it can be done well, poorly, or usually somewhere in between.

The boat rowed beautifully. It's a foot shorter and 25 pounds lighter than the fiberglass dories we're both used to, and its trimmer lines and higher rocker put proportionately less of its surface area in the water, so it's noticeably quicker and more agile. And there's an intuitive rightness about a boat made from a naturally buoyant material that just makes it seem livelier. It occurs to you not only that these drift boats derived from the original Mackenzie River dories are the pinnacle of more than a century's worth of thinking about rowing in current, but that the boat in general was one of mankind's great ideas.

Late in a float you sometimes begin to wonder about having trusted your truck and trailer to an anonymous shuttle driver based on nothing but a phone call. Did he get sick or hungover and not show up? Did he have an accident or break down? I mean, who *is* this guy anyway? Or maybe some enterprising car thief understood that your truck parked at the put-in would be unlocked with the keys and some money hidden in one of the usual places—the ash tray, cup holder, or glove box—and decided to steal it. For that matter, did you remember to tell the driver to leave it at the right takeout? It almost always works, but shit does happen, and if for some reason the shuttle didn't get run, you're in a world of hurt in the middle of nowhere with no cell phone signal and night coming on.

Vince was back on the oars when we came in sight of the rusty iron bridge above the takeout. I reeled in and nipped off my fly as we bobbed down the choppy main current under the bridge and then tucked neatly into the eddy at the boat ramp on river right. And there was the familiar truck; the only one in the lot.

101

11.

THE MARTHA STEWART
OF FLY-FISHING

I've taken my periodontist fishing a few times. (Simply put, if your dentist is the person who takes care of your teeth, your periodontist is the one who keeps those teeth in your head in the first place.) I didn't purposefully set out to find a periodontist who was also a fly-fisher; it just happened in the seemingly random way that like-minded people bump into each other more often than you'd think they would through chance alone. Coincidentally, his name is also John.

This connection didn't exactly make us best friends overnight, but the shared frame of reference did illuminate what would otherwise have been a pleasant enough, but otherwise purely professional relationship. For instance, our appointments always begin with the usual questions about where we've fished lately and what we've caught, and sometimes one or the other of us will whip out a snapshot of an especially nice fish. There's nothing competitive in this—it isn't like every fish has to outdo the last—it's just that we've both long since learned to save our bragging for those who might be impressed.

So that's how it happened that when I needed some expensive oral surgery done and my eyes bugged out when I learned how much it would cost, John said, "I'll tell you what, why don't you just take me fishing and we'll call it even." Of course I recognized the offer as charity disguised as barter in order to preserve my pride as well as my teeth, but I took him up on it anyway.

Taking someone fishing isn't the same as guiding—it's less formal, no money changes hands, and you'll be fishing yourself instead of hovering nearby like a valet with a landing net. But then it's also similar to guiding in that you'll decide where you're going, do the driving, and once there it might be up to you to suggest a fly pattern or maybe even supply one. And if you're in the proper spirit of the thing, you'll leave the best water to your guest, or at least give him first crack at it. It's also like guiding in that the success of the trip depends on you in some ill-defined but undeniable way.

The hardest people to take fishing are kids, which is why that's a chore best left to their parents. I remember being taken myself by my father and a favorite uncle beginning at—as near as the family can guess—around the age of four. I don't remember being a pain in the ass, but I must have been because at that age all kids are. They can't be left unsupervised for even a second around hazards like bodies of water, fish hooks, pocketknives, and bait that they're just as likely to play with or eat as feed to the fish. Also, they don't know anything and can't understand much, so they have to be instructed constantly, repeatedly, and in the simplest imaginable terms: the kind of mindless repetition that works on kids, but drives adults up a tree. But it's not their fault. Kids are clumsy by nature, easily bored or distracted, have short attention spans and no practical experience, and are still learning to deal effectively with things like gravity.

As old as the adults seemed to me then, they were barely out of their twenties, had young, pretty wives, and had already been through a lot. They'd grown up during the Great Depression, gone off to fight in a world war, and were now back home with their shoulders to the wheel, building families and careers and accumulating responsibilities, of which I was one. I was the quintessential baby boomer, born late in 1946, almost nine months to the day after Dad got home from the war. That's a story I could never tell while Mom was alive because the racy implication of it made her blush.

These were busy, hardworking men who deserved a little leisure and it's a fair bet that they didn't really look forward to dragging a kid along on the rare days when they had the time to go fishing. But a kid had to be taught certain manly skills, like how to fish, and if they wouldn't do it, who would? At least I was gullible enough to watch my bobber and keep quiet so I didn't "scare the fish." It would be a few years yet before I'd start to wonder why *I* had to be quiet, while the men could not only talk freely, but laugh louder, more often, and in a raunchier way than they ever did at home around their wives and daughters. I wondered what was so funny, but their sidelong glances in my direction told me I wasn't supposed to know.

If you can weather the boredom of soaking bait at a tender age they'll say you took to fishing like a duck to water, but it comes more naturally to some than to others. There are those who can't stand the inherent uncertainty of it, or the glacial pace, or who are intimidated by the knowledge that there's another intelligence involved with an agenda that's the opposite of theirs, so even if they do everything right it's still not a sure thing.

And although fishing with a fly rod isn't as hard as some make it out to be, it does add extra difficulties. At least in the beginning, fly casting seems counterintuitive and all that line in the air occasionally gets the best of even those you'd have to call experts. When people ask me about it I say that if you're not naturally patient or if you're one of those people who can't stand for things to be all tangled up, this is not your sport. Or as the motto of a fly shop in Minneapolis called Mend Provisions puts it, "Fly-fishing is hard, think twice."

I've only taught two people to fly-fish, but so far I'm batting a thousand, not because I'm a good teacher, but because they were both good students. One was a lifelong bait and spin fisherman with great fish sense who didn't forget everything he knew just because he'd gotten his hands on a different kind of tackle. The other simply had a mind sharp enough to sort out and follow my imperfect instructions, plus the kind of thoughtless physicality that made it come naturally. A few casting lessons on the grass and a little time on a stream to illustrate how moving water differs from a lawn and they were both in business. Almost overnight they went from the kind of people you *take* fishing to the kind you go fishing *with*.

Usually I'm taking a friend from out of town as part of a long-running economy of favors offered and returned until neither of us knows or cares who's ahead. Most of these folks already know how to fish as well as I do—if not better—so all I have to do is pick where we'll go, but that decision keeps me awake at night. Do I shoot for the closest you can come in fishing to a sure bet or take the long shot? Will planted rainbows do, or should we hold out for wilder trout? Do I pick a spot where if we can catch 'em at all we'll catch 'em on dry flies or go someplace where we might have to dredge nymphs to find fish? Will normal, pan-size trout do, or would they rather take a chance on fewer but bigger fish?

And what about season, stream flow, weather, the timing of hatches, and all the other things that are out of my control, like water managers who'll blow up a river in the middle of the Pale Morning Duns because folks downstream want to water their lawns and flush their toilets? All I can do is take my best shot, keep at least one backup plan in my hip pocket, and trust that if it doesn't work out my guest will understand. It's not that I aspire to be the Martha Stewart of fly-fishing; it's just that when you take someone fishing you want things to go well. After all, you're playing the role of the local fisherman who knows the score, so if nothing else you don't want to embarrass yourself.

And then there's the matter of lunch. Usually I'll make sandwiches at home—nothing fancy, though maybe a step up from peanut butter on white bread—but sometimes we'll stop somewhere along the way. As the host it'll be up to me because my guest doesn't know where to eat any more than he knows where to fish. Given the kind of out-of-the-way places we go, we often don't have a lot of choices, so we have to make due. I think it was Jim Harrison who said you should never eat at a place with gas pumps out front, although if I remember right, even he made an exception for French truck stops.

A lot depends on who you're with. When my friend Oliver comes to visit I know that he dearly loves fly-fishing for trout and is pretty good at it, but that he lives in a suburb of Paris and doesn't get out as often as he'd like. He also once told me that most of the fly fishermen he knows in France will say they had a good year if they landed six or seven trout, so I try to take him to places where, if everything goes well, he'll land twice that many in an afternoon. So far, everything has gone well and his happiness is infectious.

The first time I took Oliver fishing we made a quick stop one day for hot dogs at a Shell gas station on the drive from one stream to another. At the time he assured me that he "adored" American junk food, but later he joked with a friend about how I'd had the gall to feed a Frenchman roller dogs for lunch. So on his next visit I made sandwiches with fresh bakery bread, good deli roast beef, Havarti cheese, and the kind of spicy mustard that clears your sinuses. He said they were "okay."

The last time my friend Ed came out I decided to take him to a big pool I'd discovered high up on a small stream near home. I'd done well enough there twice before to make me reconsider my opinion that the fishing here isn't as good as it used to be. It was the kind of place you keep to yourself for a while, and then grudgingly share with certain close friends with the knowledge—or at least the hope—that they'd eventually share such a thing with you. I even orchestrated the day to heighten the effect by ducking off the trail far enough downstream that we could work our way up through pocket water that held some lesser, but still good pools and leave the big one I had in mind for the late afternoon finale.

It would have been a solid plan, but this was late September of a drought year and the creek was uncharacteristically low, clear, and bony. Furthermore, it was one of those brilliant days we get in the fall with the high-altitude sun blazing in a cloudless afternoon sky: the kind of conditions that make even wild trout almost uncatchably spooky. By fishing small flies on long, fine leaders and even longer casts, we managed to eke out a few small trout, but even being as careful and stealthy as we could, fish would sometimes explode away from our casts like shrapnel.

I'd been trying to imagine what the big pool would look like in this low flow and as it turned out I called it about right. It was shallower and narrower than I remembered, with once-submerged cobbles lying bleached and dry on the inside bend, and the gushing riffle at its head reduced to a dribble. The best we could manage were a couple of small browns and brookies. I wondered if the pool had been discovered and fished-out in the six weeks since I'd seen it last, although it seemed more likely that the big fish had simply gone wherever it is they go when you can't find them. The high-water stains were clearly visible on the rocks and Ed said he could picture what it must look like and imagine how good it would be on a cloudy day and with a better head of water. He was being gracious. I'd built this place up a little and he could see how disappointed I was.

Before long we were sitting on the exposed roots of a huge En-gelmann spruce, ostensibly resting the water for another try, but really just talking away the rest of the afternoon the way we'd talked away so many others before. We must have resembled two of those codgers you sometimes see sitting together on a park bench, going over the same ground for the hundredth time as if they were still searching for the car keys they'd lost in 1962.

The first time I took John (the periodontist) fishing, we went to a trout lake on a lease I used to belong to. This was a sprawling, shallow reservoir that was dammed up ages ago to capture spring water for the stock on a working ranch and that has since been turned into a weedy, buggy fish pond full of fat rainbows that could be real particular about what they'd eat. It was rare to hook a trout under 16 inches long there, the biggest one I ever landed measured 29 inches, and there was a legendary 10-pounder that some claimed to have seen, but that no one had ever even hooked, let alone landed.

I didn't know it then, but this place was on its way out and it was on that trip that I noticed what, in hindsight, turned out to be the first ominous signs. This was the summer after the thousand-year flood of 2013 that, along with all the other damage it did, had rearranged the water table in such a way that the springs feeding the lake were beginning to go dry. It didn't happen all at once, but the day John and I went out there I noticed that the big springs weren't running as hard as usual for that time of year and a few of the smaller ones weren't running at all.

I didn't think much of it at the time, but within a year the springs would give out entirely, the lake would warm up, the trout would begin to die off, and I'd drop out of the lease, but that day the place fished as well as ever and we caught trout as if there was no tomorrow. Some of them were nice and big, but John lost his biggest fish. I won't guess at its size, but he'd landed some over 20 inches and this one was larger still. When John set the hook, the fish shook its head ponderously for a few seconds, made one long run toward the middle of the lake, and then headed straight for a lone fence post in the shallows, where it deftly wrapped John's leader and broke off. What that post was doing out in the water is anyone's guess. The American West is littered with these steel T-posts sunk in places that must have made sense once, but are now real head-scratchers.

The next time I took John out I hired a guide to float us for a Green Drake hatch and it couldn't have gone better. We launched the raft at an improvised put-in and dawdled through the late morning while we waited for the main event. This was the kind of casual fishing that does occupy your attention, but still leaves enough room to notice and appreciate the lovely little river we were on, the steep canyon it flowed through, and the pleasantly warm summer day.

We saw our first big mayflies more or less on schedule and within fifteen minutes the fish had begun to rise to them. From there on out we caught trout at a steady clip on hair wings, feather wings, emergers, wet flies, and whatever. A fish that wouldn't take one fly would usually take another and those that wouldn't take anything could be ignored because there were so many others to cast to.

Sometimes we fished the passing seams and pockets from the

raft and sometimes we stopped to wade-fish runs where there were lots of fish working. We were in the thick of the hatch for a good four or five hours and when the mayflies finally petered out we were no more than a quarter mile from the takeout, so we could reel in, relax, and enjoy the view for that last half hour while crowing a little about what fine fishermen we were. There's a lesson in storytelling here: it's hard to build narrative tension when everything goes right.

Long story short, it was as close to a perfect day of trout fishing as you're likely to see in the real world. Even lunch was good and as I bit into my deli sandwich on its hard roll with my solid, useful teeth, I was reminded again of my debt to John, but even that had begun to feel less like an obligation and more like just one more excuse to go fishing.

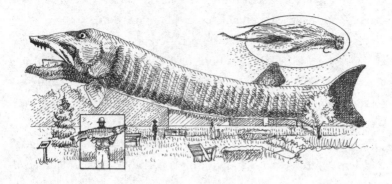

12.

THE WAY IT SHOULD HAVE BEEN

A late September morning on the north fork of the Flambeau River in Wisconsin: cool, drizzly, and windless with a low, pewter-colored sky. You couldn't ask for better fishing weather and at the put-in I was feeling expansive when our guide, Luke Swanson, asked me the loaded question, "So, how big a fly can you throw?" I knew that fall muskies like big flies—the bigger the better, according to some— and that the wrong answer would get me a sissy fly that would be easier to cast all day, but less effective. So I said something like, "I can throw whatever you got, kid."

Luke opened a custom-made fly box the size of a suitcase in

which large flies hung vertically like coats in a closet. He selected one that was heavily dressed with bucktail and saddle hackles and about a foot long, clipped it to the wire leader on a 12-weight fly rod, and handed it over with a blank look, calling my bluff.

This was my second trip here in two years and I was convinced that I'd learned a few things about fly-fishing for muskies—nothing that would revolutionize the sport or anything, but maybe enough of the fundamentals to save me from making the same beginner's mistakes all over again.

For instance, if I hadn't exactly mastered casting these big flies, I was at least getting what I thought of as passable distance and accuracy and had developed a muscle memory for how a good water haul feels. Specifically, it feels as awkward but satisfying as lobbing a dead sucker with a nine-foot slingshot. The breakthrough came when I got over thinking this was ever going to be pretty.

Setting hard enough on a strike would remain to be seen. These fish are notoriously difficult to hook and raising the rod tip to set in the usual way is all but useless. Even the stiffest rod has too much flex to impart a yank vicious enough to sink the hook point, so you have to strip-set as hard as you can with the rod pointed straight at the fish. One sharp, solid pull is good, but more would be better— whatever you have the time and the nerves for. Only then can you lean hard into the stiff spring of the rod to control an angry fish that could be as long as 50 inches. Every guide has his own way of imparting the importance of this to sports who are new to muskies. The morning before I'd overheard one of them telling a client, "If you break a rod on a fish today, I'll be proud of you."

You also want to keep the fish close, play it hard, and land it quickly. Long runs are pretty, but they only give the fish more room to get you in a snag and they also take precious time, during which it could throw the hook. I'd heard that same guide say, "If you hook dinner that night and the next morning he woke up sick. ...y, feverish, couldn't keep food down, the full catastrophe. ...in bed for the next two days with the flu and as soon as we ...he wouldn't have to go to a hospital, we started kidding him ...y landing that big musky had damn near killed him.

...he ways musky fishing reminds me of Spey casting for steel-...Atlantic salmon. It's not as elegant and it lacks the stodgy ...radition, but it does involve the same kind of attentive rep-...at you have to pace yourself for, sort of like digging a long ...entically spaced post holes. The idea of hooking a fish never ...ur mind, but the job at hand becomes one of covering water ...emingly endless series of adequate casts and retrieves.

...etimes accuracy is helpful because muskies like to tuck up ...cover like brush piles, logs, and rocks. The splat of the big, ...y hitting the water is unavoidable, but even if it weren't you'd ...yway. Muskies are lateral line ambush hunters that sense the ...ns of prey with organs that amount to long, narrow ears run-...e length of their bodies from gills to tail. The noise the fly ...hitting the water could be the struggling of an injured sucker ...ething helpless falling in the river and sometimes draws a ...false charge called a "reaction strike."

...e standard strip is a series of short, hard pulls, each one fol-...by a rest just long enough to let the fly begin to sink and the ...als seem to breathe. When done correctly, the strip is hard ...h that some have taken to wearing latex stripping guards on ...st two fingers of their rod hands to avoid rope burn. Most ...fishermen in this bunch like big flies with flat faces made of ...y spun hair that are intentionally trimmed slightly off center ...t with each pull the fly darts sideways to mimic a wounded or ...ented baitfish. So what you get is that angular scoot, followed ...low, rolling sink with the saddle hackles trailing like a silk scarf.

one, don't give it any line at all." In my limited experience I wondered if that was strictly possible, but I understood the strategy. If you tell someone not to give the fish *any* line he at least won't give it much. And there was something revealing in that "if": *if* you hook one; not *when*.

The year before I'd done it right once and remembered how good it felt. I'd also done it wrong once and learned that even if you weren't entirely skunked, it's still possible to fly home from a musky trip feeling the sting of a failed seduction. Naturally the time I did it wrong was on the biggest musky and these fish are so elusive that you can cast for hours, days, or weeks without seeing one. Any encounter at all is newsworthy, so not only is a blown strike a tragedy you'll have to live with, but everyone in camp will hear about it.

Bob White talked me into this the first time, but it didn't take a lot of talking. There's a kind of fatal attraction to fishing that demands infinite patience followed by grace under pressure, both of which you assume you have in you if you can dig deep enough when the time comes. You know you'll be inept at first and you hope to learn the ropes before you lose heart. Then, on the flight home, you sift through the wreckage of that big missed fish, not wondering what you did wrong because you know what you did wrong, but pondering why you did it when you knew better. You won't make the call for months yet, but this is the precise moment when the return trip begins.

Musky fishing has been going on in northern Wisconsin for as long as people have been fishing here, including the people of the Ojibway Nation. (The fish's proper name, muskellunge, is said to be an Anglo mispronunciation of an Ojibway word.) If you look through the world records you'll see a long list of Wisconsin locations with token appearances from other places like Minnesota and Ontario scattered here and there. And although nearby Hayward isn't the only place in the state that bills itself as the Musky Capital of the World, it's the only one with a four-story-tall statue of one that you catch disconcerting glimpses of as you drive around town.

Most of that fishing was done with conventional tackle and either big plugs or big bait. Fly-fishing for muskies is a fairly recent development, but that's not to say no one ever tried it before about twenty-five years ago. In his book *Musky on the Fly*, Robert Tomes reproduced a sepia-tone photo from the 1920s of one William Vogt holding what Tomes says might be the first musky ever caught on a fly. The rod is identified as a three-and-a-half-ounce split bamboo with "a light test line," so you have to wonder if this was either a stunt or a mistake. The fish weighed 30 pounds and in the photo Vogt looks not only happy, but also surprised.

People fly-fishing for pike would have inevitably hooked muskies from time to time and the same goes for bass fishermen, especially early in the season when muskies are more likely to feed on the same smaller prey a bass would eat. It's easy to see how that would get a certain kind of hairy-chested fly caster thinking about stepping up to saltwater fly rods and billfish flies, which is supposedly how all this got started. But much of that went on in the golden age before social media when fishermen who were on to something were smart enough to keep quiet about it, so records are scarce.

By now fly-fishing for muskies is well known enough that most fly fishermen have heard about it, although they've probably never done it and may not even want to. It's gone mainstream enough that some tackle companies are now marketing 8-, 9-, and 10-weight musky rods, although most of the musky guides I've talked to would rather have an 11- or 12-weight tarpon rod in the boat.

Some of the musky flies I've seen for sale also seem a little on the small side, but that's probably just because of this bunch I've been hanging out with. (The first time I went I brought my biggest pike

and lake trout flies, but was told the of these guys want the biggest flies have been reengineering large flies others have been building up spinnin casting as fly rods and loading them throw flies up to 20 inches long.

Earlier that month back home i mountain creek with a friend and caug unbelievable pig for this small, high alt ing with the news when I got to Wis came to tell the story to some of the who cast 20-inch flies for 50-inch fish m for an 18-inch trout.

So fly-fishing for muskies is beginn ticles in the magazines and new conver the fly-fishing guides working now aren't fly-caught muskies, they may be the first to specialize in it. On the other hand, the clusive feel to it and some practitioners h titude of those who feel misunderstood ev far the rivers aren't crowded with fly-fisher you wonder how much longer that can last.

The fishing that week seemed slow, bu of us had fishless days without so much as fish were seen, moved or caught by someo one guy landed a whopping 49¾-inch musl that was only a quarter inch short of the co would make it an official trophy. I overheard saying that if it were him, he'd have roundec inches even. No one would have argued, least

But then the poor guy who caught that fish

It really does look like something dying overdramatically in the third act of an opera.

I knew I still had plenty to learn and tried to stay open to it. I had my beginner's simple opinions about flies, but if a guide suggested one I didn't think much of I'd fish it hard anyway, hoping to learn something new. You have to have some faith in your guide. He might hand you a new fly that's never caught a fish before, but unless you've really rubbed him the wrong way, he won't give you one that he knows for sure won't work.

It was all going smoothly until one night after dinner when some people started discussing politics. You should understand that this is frowned upon. There's an unwritten law at fish camps that politics and religion are taboo, and for good reason. Everyone there has two opinions in common: that trying to catch fish is a worthwhile way to spend your spare time and money and that how to go about catching them is an endlessly fascinating and inexhaustible subject. There's a fair chance that most of you will never see each other again and none of you came on this trip expecting to defend your beliefs, so why muddy the water? That was especially true in September 2016 when everyone's politics, like the presidential campaign itself, had begun to escalate from the usual anger to something resembling rage.

Still, someone who just couldn't help himself piped up with something mildly provocative and a visible wave of discomfort circled the table. People shifted uneasily in their chairs, throats were cleared, the man next to me stared into his three fingers of Maker's Mark as if he'd just found a fly floating in it.

I don't remember the particulars—it had all become white noise by then—but I do remember that those who spoke up first seemed aware they were breaking a cardinal rule and so were careful to the point of being apologetic. (That's how it always starts.) Others kept quiet, including the guides who understood that inadvertently pissing off a client would not only be pointless, but could also adversely affect their tips.

I kept quiet myself, although I nearly had to chew off my own tongue to do it, and my photographer friend Mike Dvorak, knowing I have a short political fuse and opinions eclectic enough to let me pick a fight with anyone, kept glancing at me as if I were a hand grenade whose pin had just been pulled. I didn't want this trip to turn into *Fear and Loathing in Northern Wisconsin*, so I decided it was best to step outside for a literal and figurative breath of fresh air.

The night was chilly and still, with the moon casting a silver rind around the clouds that covered it. I walked down to the bank of the Chippewa River and listened to the purling of its current for a few minutes. There, that's better. I read that once upon a time in India insane people were tied to trees on the banks of rivers so the sound of moving water could draw out their madness. I wondered if we had enough rivers and enough trees to give every registered voter in America the same treatment.

It had all blown over by the next day when I fished with Dan Boggs, who taught me a neat trick for my figure-8: the maneuver you perform at the end of every retrieve hoping any musky that shadowed the fly this far out of curiosity will think it's getting away and be induced to strike. It happens more often than you'd think.

I told Dan that last year I'd been using the final swing of the figure-8 as a water haul to pick up for the next cast, but that once when I did that I snatched the fly away from a huge musky with jaws that could have swallowed a cantaloupe. Dan said to make the last swing from deep to shallow and then stop the fly right at the surface in what he called a "death stall." If there *is* an unseen musky following the fly, he might grab it, or at least loom up out of the depths and reveal his presence while the fly is still in the water and you can try something else.

Her presence, actually. The big muskies everyone is after—the ones over 40 inches—are almost always females.

I went out with Luke on my last day. I was fully aware that in the morning I'd head down to the airport in Minneapolis and fly home, where I no doubt had important things to do, but I don't recall feeling any particular sense of urgency. It's possible to reach a point on a fishing trip where time no longer matters in the usual way and that's especially true when you're after what people like to call a fish of a thousand casts, or sometimes they'll say *ten* thousand, just to drive the point home. You simply make each cast with the identical sense of purpose as the last one, not feeling the least bit misunderstood, but aware that you could never explain how beautiful this is to someone who doesn't already get it.

By early afternoon it was raining just hard enough to have the hood up on my rain slicker. I'd made yet another cast with that same big fly and was figure-eighting it at the boat when the line came tight. There was no live thump or yank, everything just stopped, and even as I set as hard as I could I thought, *This feels like a snag, but better safe than sorry.*

On the musky's first run it pulled out all the line I'd stripped off for my cast and a few more turns off the reel before I got it stopped. From there on out I never gave another inch of line and began to gain some back. A good-size musky looks like a fish that could be too big to land, but in fact they're built for short, predatory bursts of speed, not for endurance, so if you fight them as violently as they're fighting you ("If you break a rod on a fish today I'll be proud of you") it's possible to get them to the boat pretty quickly.

Bob and Mike had been following along in another boat, fishing the opposite bank, and by the time Luke got the fish in the net they'd rowed over to have a look at it. (Catching a musky is such a unique event that it draws whatever crowd is available.) This was a female that taped out at precisely 47¼ inches and seemed so big and unwieldy that at first I didn't know how to hold it for the obligatory photos that would be shown around camp as soon as we got back. I wanted to look heroic and competent, but I felt more like a monkey wrestling with a fire hose.

That evening at the lodge, with my bags packed to go in the morning, Mike and I were lounging in big easy chairs having the usual last-night-in-camp conversation. A fishing trip is more about the process than the result, but the end of one still demands that final paragraph that begins, "And so, as the sun sinks slowly in the west . . ." There was still a knot of guys lingering at the dinner table with drinks and I overheard one of them say, "Just goes to show that even a guy who's fished as long as he has can still come unglued over a big musky."

They couldn't have been talking about me, could they? The way I remembered it—and the way I'd told it more than once that evening—I'd more or less done everything right, from the awkward but effective set right under the boat to steering the fish into the waiting net, and never once "come unglued." Of course Luke would have told the same story and, being the guide and all, his version would have rightly been taken as the true account. But truth is subjective and whenever I hear a fish story—or tell one for that matter—I remember an old western movie that began with the epigraph, "If this ain't the way it was, it's at least the way it should have been."

13.

RUNOFF

I grew up among sensible midwestern lake fishermen who didn't much care for rivers and streams. Moving water was too unruly, forever arriving and departing like time itself and prone to seasonal personality disorders that made it unpredictable. My people weren't exactly dour, but as Germanic heart-landers they were suspicious of the kinds of surprises kids and rivers regularly served up. They expected their children and their water to stand still and behave and at least the lakes didn't disappoint them.

So I didn't develop a taste for current until I moved west after college, and as with some of my other newly acquired appetites, I fell hard. The restlessness of streams matched the mood of my early twenties, and the enormity of their courses from snowmelt creeks to rivers to brackish tidewater to clouds that dropped more snow in the mountains was the kind of big idea I was learning to like. For that matter, after a childhood of bass lurking beneath lily pads, trout seemed impossibly quick and flawless, darting and hovering like UFOs in currents that must feel like a constant wind. I quickly came to love everything about streams—except runoff.

Even after more than enough time in Colorado to get used to it, I'm still discouraged by a mountain trout stream in full spring flood, rumbling with current, and opaque with mud and mats of beige foam whipped to a froth by plunge pools. Staring at this brown mess, the perky little size 16 dry flies I hope to be fishing here in six weeks seem unlikely to ever be useful again. I remind myself that in the mountains snow is life itself and that when it melts it has to go somewhere; also that trout eat well and grow fat in high water and that when the streams finally drop and clear the fish will be chubby and gullible, but it doesn't help. Maybe I wouldn't go fishing every day of my life even if I could, but I don't see why I shouldn't be able to.

The spotty pre-runoff fishing here begins as early as the occasional warm spells in March. With the headwaters still locked in snow, the low country streams are clear and perfect, and although the water is often too cold for fishing, it sometimes warms enough on sunny afternoons to trigger brief hatches of small, hardy aquatic insects. When that happens it's possible to actually catch a trout on a dry fly—a fresh miracle after a winter that's dragged on too long. I try to get out whenever things seem promising to warm up my casting arm and work out the off-season kinks, but I know it's borrowed time and I fret about the fishing as if it were a degenerative medical condition. How many good days do I have left? No telling, but not as many as I'd like.

Some years runoff begins gradually enough to provide fair warning—the current is a little swifter today than it was last week; it's getting harder to see my wading boots clearly at a depth of two feet—but this spring the reprieve ended abruptly with an early heat wave. One day the weather was cool and the streams were still clear and inviting; a few days later it was 92 in the shade, the mountain snowpack was melting off in buckets, and every creek on the Front Range was out of its banks with muddy snowmelt. This ice water looked inviting on those first hot days and it was, but only for the twenty seconds it took for your bare feet to first sting and then go numb. If you were smart, you quickly got over any ideas you might have had about jumping in for a quick, refreshing swim, but not everyone is smart and we lost some overeager tubers to drowning exacerbated by hypothermia and, often enough to mention, large quantities of beer. Fast-water rescue types saw that as a preventable tragedy ("when will they learn?") while others shrugged it off as natural selection.

Runoff lasts as long as it lasts, depending on how much snow fell in the mountains the previous winter and how long it takes to melt. It's usually around six weeks in a normal year, during which fly fishers are said to go quietly mad from frustration, but in fact most of us handle it well enough. We either look after our own affairs—which usually benefit from all the attention we can spare—or we travel somewhere more promising. Someone once said that the fish are always biting somewhere, even if it's in another hemisphere. That presupposes a large travel budget and lots of leisure time, but it's still good to know.

The streams around home were unrecognizable in May when I fled to Montana with my friend Ed Engle to attend an event at the Montana State University Library. There was a tour and reception, followed by a good dinner, and then Thomas McGuane gave a talk titled "Does Fishing Mean Anything?" (He thought it did.) The next day we fished the Madison River even though it had recently gone into its own runoff. When we got to the river the water was high and muddy and the thirty-mile-an-hour downstream wind smelled of smoke from a wildfire in Alberta, but we were there and had already bought nonresident fishing licenses. Late in the day we finally eked out a few small browns on Woolly Buggers from a creek-like side channel, so technically we weren't skunked.

We pulled it out the following day on Nelson's Spring Creek, where we fished with Doug and Bill, two friends and former guide clients of Ed's. When we paid our rod fees Mary Nelson asked if we needed to buy any flies and Doug nodded at the bins and said, "We already have more flies between us than this shop does." That was good for a laugh, but then out on the water I wondered if we'd been too hasty. The stream was glass-clear and trout were picking at a multiple hatch of midges and mayflies in the desultory way of over-fed housecats, each with its own peculiar idea about what it wanted to eat. The hatch went on for hours and I went through yards of tippet in the course of changing out every fly I had in a size 18 or smaller. I did catch fish, but never more than two or three on any one pattern, and could never shake the idea that I was only hooking the dumb ones.

Later Doug and Bill cooked us a fine dinner at their rented cabin and then we drove back to our motel in Livingston. Those guys were good fishermen and Ed said he finally realized he was learning as much from them as they were from him, so they dropped the whole guide/client pretense and just started fishing together.

Back home I pushed my luck when runoff finally began to sub-side a little, getting out while friends were still saying they should go fishing soon but hadn't gotten around to it yet. I *was* eager, but there was also the thought that if I sniffed something out I could play the role of the crafty hometown fisherman with the first good tip of the season. At certain times of the year we fishermen congratulate ourselves on our legendary patience and then burn appalling amounts of fossil fuel looking for fishable water.

I tried the least of the local tributaries, a pretty little creek that drains a smaller mountain basin than the others and so comes down out of runoff sooner. The bad news is that this creek then goes on to get so low later in the year that trout much bigger than 9 inches can't winter over. But so be it. When you haven't caught a trout in almost a month, 9-inchers will get the job done.

I parked at the dirt road turnout, strung up a 4-weight rod, and hiked down the narrow canyon while a thunderstorm passed to the northwest, out of sight behind the ridge, but still within earshot. It was the beginning of monsoon season with its usually harmless but sometimes monstrous mountain storms, and the not-so-distant thunder reminded me of the official advice about flash floods—"climb to safety"—as well as the unspoken footnote—"If you have time."

This happened to be the day after England voted to leave the European Union, which some predicted would have disastrous effects on the world economy. On the drive to the stream the radio news reported on the shock wave traveling around the global stock markets with the time zones and arriving that very morning in New York. Then, after using the word "panic" five times in the previous twenty minutes, they trotted out a financial expert with a deep, comforting voice who warned people not to panic. I wondered if I should be back in town cashing out my modest investments, but then realized it was already too late, while down in the canyon the thought of a threat as unambiguous as a flash flood was almost a relief. If the worst happened my only decision would be whether to scramble out of the canyon carrying my favorite bamboo fly rod or leave it behind so I could use both hands.

The stream was still running a little high, but had dropped enough to reveal fishable slicks and eddies and was clear enough that I could see the bottom in all but the deepest holes. I fished a soft hackle dropper behind a dry fly made mostly of closed-cell foam and rug fibers, a pattern chosen more for buoyancy and visibility than for its plausibility as an insect. In other words, a bobber that lets you fish a nymph while pretending you're dry fly-fishing.

It was late afternoon when I finally took a lunch break in a stand of ponderosa pines that had grown straight and tall out of the dark canyon and crowned out in the sun as if they were holding up the sky. I'd seen three other people that day. One was a fly fisherman who spotted me from the trail forty feet up the far side of the canyon, where he waved and pointed, indicating that he'd get in downstream and leave me the water ahead. The other two were hikers who either didn't see me at all or did a fine job of ignoring me as they clipped by logging steps on their Fitbits.

By then I'd caught around a dozen fish, all the descendants of the brown trout that had been stocked there generations ago and had long since gone wild. Most were small, but a few were as big as they get here, which is all you can ask for. I carefully put them all back as usual, but still had a little pang of nostalgia for keeping some fish. I don't do that much anymore and when I do I like them to be bigger, but I always liked the sense of accomplishment that comes with a stringer of trout, not to mention the symbolic neighborliness of giving some away. It's a small gift that could act as a reciprocation of past favors or a come-on for future ones, as well as a backhanded way of saying, "I can spare a few because I have plenty and can always get more; I'm that good a fisherman." I like them butterfly-filleted and fried with salt, garlic, and butter and it was that memory that finally made me stop to eat my peanut butter sandwich.

I spent the next few weeks reexploring my home water as the streams dropped, working up toward what I think of as the sweet spot in the high country, where the season is desperately short. At these elevations it's sometimes only a month between the end of runoff and the first frosts that shrivel the wildflowers and send the hummingbirds to Guatemala. In early falls when the fishing shuts down with startling suddenness I always feel cheated, regardless of how many times I got out. The old-timers here used to say, "If summer falls on a weekend, we'll have a picnic" and long before that the Arapahos gave a nearby range a name that roughly translates as "the Never Summer Mountains."

As soon as the water came down enough I went to my favorite creek. This isn't necessarily the best stream in the region—although it has its moments—but it's the one I've fished the longest and felt I knew the best until the flood of 2013 rearranged the drainage. This one held up better than some of the streams at lower elevations because it carried a smaller head of water, but it still took a hit and the first time I went there after the flood was like visiting a friend who'd just gotten out of rehab and finding her to be the same person, but shell-shocked and distracted.

There were noticeably fewer fish than there used to be, but since the survivors had less competition for food, they were unusually fat that first summer after the flood. And what had once been brown trout water now held mostly brook trout, while the water a few miles upstream that we used to call the Brookie Stretch was now populated by cutthroats that had moved down from above to fill the vacuum. The stream itself looked more or less the same, not counting some good log jam pools that had washed out and some once-productive channels that had either moved or filled in with sand. I could fish along for a while on an entirely recognizable creek, only to get disoriented in a stretch that had become unrecognizable.

This was now the third summer since the flood. There were getting to be some nice-size trout again and fingerlings with parr marks were beginning to show up as evidence that they were spawning. The creeks this high in the drainage had so far been spared by the chronically impatient fish stockers and habitat improvers, so things were progressing nicely at their own natural pace.

One day I decided to try a stream I like in the national park, which may have been a mistake. There were enough cars that I had trouble finding a place to park and enough people on the trail that as I took my place in the crowd of hikers I had to be careful not to poke someone's eye out with my rod tip. This was my first time there this season, but I knew it was the hundred-year anniversary of a popular national park and gas was cheap that summer, so what did I expect?

Most fishermen here like the two miles or so of meandering meadow that stretch downstream with its deeply cut bend pools, open grassy banks where elk come to graze in the evenings, and a clear view of Stones Peak to the west. I prefer the pocket water above where the stream steepens and straightens, and pine, spruce, and aspen close in. I got in above the footbridge on the trail where, I hoped, I'd leave the hikers and most of the fishermen behind.

The stream hadn't yet dropped to that ideal flow I envision over the winter as I haul in another armload of firewood, but it was clear and passably well defined and the fish were looking up. It's still mostly browns and brook trout here as it always was, although since the flood some cutthroats have been turning up, possibly washed down from Forest Canyon. I caught browns and brookies and a few were just big enough to put a deep bend in the light rod and even pull a turn or two of line off the little reel. This particular stream came back faster and better than any of the others and now has bigger trout than it did before the flood. At first I thought I'd eventually be able to work out why, but so far no such luck.

I'd fished slowly upstream for an hour or so when I came around a bend and spotted another fisherman ahead of me. He spotted me, too, although he pretended he hadn't, and immediately headed upstream at a fast walk so I couldn't get in ahead of him. I shrugged and started on a wide loop, intending to leave him a few pools before I got back in the water, but at the next run he spotted me through the trees and rushed ahead again, reeling in as he went.

This does happen from time to time, although so far it's still the exception. My best guess is that these water hogs are adult-onset fishermen who didn't grow up with their elders drilling them on how to behave on the stream and so don't understand the rules, although I have other, less generous theories.

Or maybe it's just that there are too many people now, especially in these popular and well publicized destinations, so that traditional courtesy is gradually being replaced by a kind of ruthless Darwinism. This park gets on the order of three million visitors every year and the population of Colorado has more than doubled in the forty-eight years since I moved here. Politicians and Chambers of Commerce think that's nothing but a good start, while locals continue to find out-of-state fishermen standing in their secret pools.

Of course by "too many people" I mean that my friends and I are okay, but there are too many of you *other* people.

I do feel some of the authority of a tenured local after nearly half a century of continuous residence, but there are some who reserve that venerable title for those who were not only born here, but can trace their ancestry back to homesteaders with Civil War surplus rifles stuffed in their saddle scabbards. You can spot some of them by the bumper stickers on their pickups that read NATIVE or, since the legalization of marijuana and the advent of pot tourism, YOU GOT HIGH NOW GO HOME. On the other hand, to fresher newcomers I manage to come off as authentically leathery and cantankerous with

131

plenty of stories about how much better things were before *they* showed up.

The way I saw it, there were two ways this could go: I could get into a passive/aggressive tussle with the guy who'd rushed ahead of me that would either turn into a pitiful sitcom or leave us both in a murderous but impotent rage, or I could go back and fish the two good pools he'd hardly touched and then hike out and drive to another stream. Runoff was all but over by then and I had my choice of half a dozen other creeks within a forty-minute drive of where I stood, all of them less crowded than this one.

The breeze was cool, the sun was warm, fair-weather cumulonimbus clouds were sailing east toward Kansas in a turquoise sky, and the fish were biting. It was, in fact, one of those perfect days that make tourists want to chuck it all and move here. I don't always respond well to rudeness on the water, but this time I remember thinking, *If you let that one asshole ruin this for you, it'll be your own fault.*

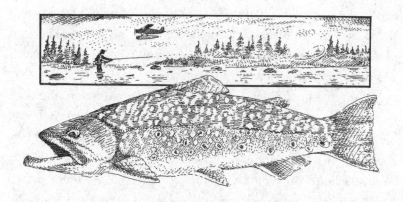

14.

LABRADOR

I'd booked Air Canada flights from Denver to Toronto to Montreal to Sept Iles, and on to Wabush, Labrador, in a single day. It was a tight schedule that invited missed connections and lost luggage, but eliminated the first of the usual two overnights with their expensive hotel rooms. This is the kind of imperfect bargain you strike while traveling—imperfect because you're just as likely to inadvertently create a new problem as you are to solve an old one.

I did end up cutting it a little close in Montreal when I made the long trek from the second of two big jets to a distant annex to catch the little twin-prop Dash 8 that would puddle-jump on north, but not as close as my friends Bob and Mike. Their flight up from Minneapolis had been breathlessly late and then they'd gotten tangled up in airport construction, missed a poorly marked detour on the way to the gate, and ended up back out in the terminal again, where they had to slog through security for a second time. It was the kind of nightmare loop that would make you wake up in a cold sweat if you were lucky enough to be dreaming.

As it turned out, they dashed on board seconds before the door closed and long after I'd written them off as lost in transit. Bob said he was glad they made it, but that he was afraid their checked luggage wouldn't, and sure enough, when we landed in Wabush that night, my duffel came out of the little plane's hold, but theirs didn't. At what passes for the baggage counter in an airport with only one gate a lady tapped on her computer for a while and then announced that she had no idea where their bags were, although her best guess was Montreal because "That's where they usually are."

Just after dawn the next morning we flew another 150 miles north by floatplane to Three Rivers Lodge, where, over a late breakfast of pancakes and bacon, the guides and other fishermen learned of the lost luggage and immediately ponied up more than enough spare gear and tackle for Bob and Mike to fish. This is the kind of thoughtful generosity that makes you think the human race might be worth saving after all.

So: back in Labrador again. I've lost track of how many times I've been here. Eight trips? Nine? Plus three trips to other lodges before I discovered this place and settled in. Whatever, it now qualifies as habitual, but given the uncertainties of life, fishing, and the lodge business, every time I leave it feels like it's for the last time and on each return trip I'm flooded with relief that it's still there.

It starts on the flight in from Wabush, skimming for almost two hours above a landscape that's more water than land, all of it lacking so much as a human footprint. Even on bright days with sunlight sparkling on the water this country looks intimidating, and when it's raining and chilly, as it was on this trip, it seems thrillingly forbidding.

Then there's the first sight of the camp's red roofs as the de Havilland Otter banks for its approach, dangling its pontoons like talons, and the dock where two golden retrievers and the entire staff are assembled, all but the dogs dressed for this semiformal occasion in matching denim shirts with the lodge logo over the breast pocket. It's the only time you'll see any of these folks in uniform.

And so it goes. There's the boardwalk made of rough-sawn spruce planks that saves you from slopping through mud, the cabin porch stacked with firewood, the door that doesn't want to latch, the bunks with their tropical-looking bug nets, the smoldering mosquito coil smelling like incense. I'm walking with Judy, who works in the kitchen with Francis, when one of the guides passes humping my gear in a two-wheeled cart. She says to him, with a good-natured leer, "Just take John's stuff to my place" and I'm quick enough on my feet to say, "Yeah, I should be so lucky."

I like this place so much that I once thought about someday having my ashes scattered here. But then I learned how many fishermen have had the same idea (it's hardly the unique gesture I'd imagined) and heard about some of the pratfalls that have ensued at other camps. Like the lodge owner who took off one day to scatter the ashes of a former client from the floatplane, but didn't foresee the backdraft that would be caused by sliding open the window of the cockpit. He radioed the head guide, asked him to meet him back at the dock with a Shop-Vac and to "Keep this to yourself."

Not long after breakfast we were in the floatplane with Robin, the lodge owner, and Gillis, our French Canadian pilot, heading to Twin Cub Run, so named because the first time they scouted it a mother bear, worried about her two cubs, made an awful fuss woofing and shaking the alders. Gillis dropped us there with the promise to pick us up that evening, adding, in his French-accented English, that the wind direction was "good for go; not so much for come back."

The walk to the run itself seemed longer than it really was because of the thick, overgrown woods, slippery caribou moss, and the clouds of mosquitos and black flies that are inevitable at this time of year. This was mid-July and we were hoping for hatches, but if you come for the flies the fish eat, you also get the flies that eat you. There are no fisherman's paths here, so we tried to pick our way along bear trails, but none of the bears had been going where we were, so it was mostly slow bushwhacking.

This was a short stretch of water with a few obvious honey holes, the kind of spot that's productive when fished slowly and occasionally rested. You might start with a size 10 Royal Wulff, then come through sometime later with a skated orange Bomber, and still later to make a final pass with a big weighted streamer.

There are a number of spots like this within floatplane range of camp, but access is the key. If you can't safely land a floatplane within reasonable walking distance, these creek-like channels draining one lake into another might as well be on the moon. The lodge doesn't bring many people to any of them and even as it is the walk is too hard for some of the older clients. (The camp manager, Kevin, once joked with Robin about promoting the camp at assisted living facilities.) And for more able-bodied fishermen who expect nonstop action, the fishing is too slow, there's not enough water, and there's too much bank sitting to rest the water that they'd consider wasted time, although it's not wasted at all. Even in a place as wild as interior Labrador with its large, ferocious brook trout, small water like this must be fished with patience and something resembling reverence.

Bob and Mike fished well wearing borrowed waders with boots that didn't quite fit, and casting donated flies with unfamiliar rods. These were perfectly serviceable fly patterns, but not the ones they'd chosen for themselves and that must have caused them some uncertainty, although they never said anything. Much is made about the efficacy of using favorite flies that you have supreme confidence in, but then there's the opposing theory that it's all about the cast and drift and the fly hardly matters. The best fishermen can switch back and forth seamlessly between these two belief systems, feeling out a sweet spot somewhere in between.

The water showed off in a nicely characteristic way for my friends' first day ever in Labrador. We didn't catch a lot of fish, which is often the case here, but they were good ones, mostly between four and six pounds with one seven-pounder I skated up on a Bomber. In something like a dozen trips to this region I can only remember a single day when my partners and I caught five- and six-pound brook trout at the rate you can sometimes achieve with 8-inchers in a Colorado beaver pond, but for the most part these fish are hard won and far between, especially the biggest ones. It's a state of affairs that jibes nicely with the midwestern Protestant ethic all three of us grew up on: the one that warns of the ruination that comes from too much of a good thing. In fact it was fishing in Labrador that finally cured me of my compulsive score-keeping. Of course it's an ongoing struggle, but whereas once I'd get envious when someone went on too long about how many fish they caught and how big they were, now the large dog that lives in my mind just rolls over and goes to sleep.

Back in camp that evening we learned that not only had Bob and Mike's duffels finally arrived from Montreal (or wherever) but that, unbelievably, the airline had chartered the lodge's floatplane and pilot to come and get them. I say "unbelievably" because floatplanes are obscenely expensive to hire and this three-hundred-mile round-trip must have cost several times what those guys paid for their tickets. My memories of flying with this airline include lots of late or canceled flights and lost luggage, but it's still probably unfair to single them out. (After all, the airline with the worst service record still invites its customers to fly the friendly skies.) In the end it reminds me of some hapless friends I've had who were chronic fuckups, but who then tried so hard to make things right that I couldn't stay mad at them.

Bob and Mike were happy to see their stuff, as anyone would be, but there was no undue celebrating, just as there'd been no excessive whining when the bags turned up missing in the first place—just the steady fatalism that every successful traveling fisherman develops as a survival tactic.

At Indian Rapids a few fish were rising in the tubs and slicks that are scattered through this otherwise uniformly fast, shallow water and they were being unusually picky. No dice on the flies that usually work: the Royal Wulff, the Brown Parachute Wulff, or the skated Stimulator. I worked down through smaller and smaller dry flies and finally connected with a brace of size 16 Hares Ear Soft Hackles swung down and across wet fly-style. I didn't know what Bob and Mike were fishing and they were too far away on this big water to yell at, but I'd see their rods bent from time to time, so it was only a matter of curiosity. None of us caught many brook trout that day, but they were all big—nothing much under six pounds and with the short, thick bodies that are typical of these northern fish.

At the bottom of the rapids late in the day I came to a midstream rock. It's the only dry rock in sight, a few steps from a big, fishy trough, and just the right easy-chair shape and height for a fisherman to sit on in order to retie a leader, study his fly box, or just contemplate the hand fate had dealt him that day. Maybe I've plopped down there more often than most because Kevin has taken to calling it

John's Rock. If the name survives Kev's tenure here, it'll be my ticket to immortality.

After dinner at camp that evening I ended up on the back porch with the usual revolving crew, which always includes one if not both dogs trolling for a handout. There's a big porch out front with comfortable chairs and a view of Crossroads Lake, but the real action is on these hard benches off the kitchen where Francis and Judy take their breaks and the guides come and go on their seemingly endless errands, all dropping in and out of the running conversation.

Newfoundlanders not only love to talk, but they're wonderfully attentive listeners, hanging on your every word and quick to laugh until you begin to think you're a natural-born storyteller. TV and the Internet have intruded as deeply into the north country as they have anywhere else, but in a culture with such an old and deep oral tradition, talking on the porch in the evening still dominates prime time.

I knew all but one of the guides because, like me, they'd been returning here for years as if to a second home. The exception was Simon, who'd been wintering in Mexico for many seasons and finally decided to stay on and go native. The new guy was Emile, a sturdy young guide who supplements his income tying some of the most flawless Atlantic salmon flies I've ever seen. His blog has many followers and the older guides are quick to point out that the majority of them are young women. I'd say that only in Labrador could a handsome young fishing guide become an Internet heartthrob, but then I might be selling Montana short.

Most of the folks here have a hobby or avocation to ease the inevitable boredom of a whole season in the bush as well as maybe bringing in a little extra cash on the side. (Clients are free to spend their entire budget of enthusiasm on a week of fishing, while those who are here for the long haul have to ration it to last the season.) These range from Emile's salmon flies to Robin and Kev hustling clients on games of horseshoes to Francis and Judy's ferocious games of cribbage to Anthony's wonderfully clunky wood carvings of craggy-looking fishermen with almost comically oversize fish that could be called primitive as long as you'd also be willing to call Picasso primitive.

The fishermen that week were the usual mixed bag of sports: the retired airline pilot, the coffee shop owner from Maine, the Defense Department consultant who seemed darkly mysterious because he couldn't talk about his work, and so on. Bob is a career guide himself and a well-known sporting artist whose paintings you've probably been seeing for years in hunting and fishing magazines. Mike is a guide and professional photographer who favors black-and-white film that he develops and prints himself in his studio in Minneapolis. You could say this was a working trip for both of them—and these are men whose work I admire—but to all outward appearances they were just fishing with expensive cameras hung around their necks like countless other tourists.

We had a slow day at Eagle River, which is just a half hour boat ride from camp and then a hike that can be long or short depending on how ambitious you are. This is big, deep, boulder-strewn, often unwadable water with a moody streak that can leave you scratching your head. I've had great days here fishing big dries and streamers and other days, like this one, when you'd swear there wasn't a fish in the river. That's a possibility. These fish are constantly on the move throughout the season and although there are dependable spots, it's possible to go to any of them and, after a few hours of casting, conclude that the fish have moved on.

Finally our guide, Michel, suggested that on the way back we stop and catch some pike. I knew this was a stretch for him because he actively hates pike and isn't shy about saying so, but he's also a pro and the need to put his people into fish by the end of the day overcame his dislike for this species. So we motored to a small, rocky bay with a creek inlet, went to work with our biggest, gaudiest streamers on wire leaders, and caught fish easily. They weren't all that large as pike go, but they were big enough to pull hard and there were lots of them, so for an hour or so it was good, simpleminded fun for everyone except Michel. Every time he'd unhook one and toss it back, he'd wipe his slimy hands on his waders and mutter, "Fookin' poik!"

Finally one of us said, "Hey, Michel, what do you say we knock off a little early today" and he had the outboard going before we could even reel in our lines. The last thing he said when we thanked him at the dock was, "*Jeez*, I hates poik!"

When we flew to Eagle's Beak in the headwaters of the Eagle River, Gillis circled repeatedly, studying the small strip of water that might be deep enough to land on and considering the wind direction. On the third or fourth pass I expected him to turn to Robin and our guide Byron and shrug. Robin would then shrug back, point off in one direction or another, and we'd go somewhere else. (I'd seen this drill before. The decision about landing safely belongs to the pilot alone and there's no room for discussion.) But then on the next pass we began to lose altitude and on the one after that the pontoons skimmed the treetops and we settled on the water, bobbing in our own wake like a goose.

Gillis dropped us off on a rubble rock shelf and we waded fifty yards to shore through thigh-deep water and entered a short, dense, scrubby black spruce forest littered with deadfall and dripping from a light but steady rain. Except for the sound of rainwater weeping from the trees, the place was utterly silent and seemed primordial, as if you wouldn't be surprised to bump into an animal here that was previously thought to be extinct.

That evening we hiked back to the lake at the appointed time to meet the plane, which was late. It was still raining, but we'd left the shelter of the trees and waded out to perch on a couple of exposed boulders to escape the worst of the mosquitos. Bob heard the plane first—"I'm good with low frequencies" he said—but it was another minute before the rest of us could make it out.

When we waded out to load up, Gillis announced that because of the wind direction and short takeoff space, he could only take three of us in the first load and would have to come back for the other two. Robin started pointing at each of us in turn saying "eenie, meenie, miney, mo," then laughed and told Bob, Mike, and me to climb aboard. He and Byron would wait for the second trip for the inarguable reason that no guide would think of flying back to dry clothes, a warm woodstove, and hot coffee while leaving clients alone in the rain. It's just not done.

Back at camp we unloaded quickly and Gillis was off again before we even left the dock, so we had to grab our hats in his prop wash. The storm was settling in, he was running late, and it was getting dark, and although the big packs all the guides carry contain some basic survival gear, it would be nowhere near enough to keep it from being a miserably long, wet, cold, hungry, buggy night. We did change into dry clothes, warm up at the stove, and get some coffee, but we couldn't relax until the plane returned right at dark and Robin and Byron sauntered up from the dock.

We'd only landed a handful of brook trout that day from a channel so short you could see the lakes at either end, but they included our two biggest. According to the standard length and girth formula—which doesn't account for the variable thickness of the wrist at the base of the tail and so isn't entirely accurate—mine weighed seven and a half pounds and Mike's came in at eight; both thick, hard, pugnacious fish that were built like miniature fireplugs. I know I claimed earlier that Labrador had cured me of scorekeeping, but I entered the weights in my notebook at the time to keep myself from exaggerating later and I'm now studying the prints Mike sent of those two fish. They somehow look more substantial in black and white, like complacently fat captains of industry posing for their portraits in a previous century. Here at my familiar desk only a few months later, it all seems impossibly long ago and far from home.

15.

THE ADAMS

I'd seen some of the evocative pencil drawings of trout flies Bob White had done on the half-title pages of books (what artists and book people call a "remarque") and when I asked him if he'd do one for me he said, "Sure, what's your favorite pattern?" I hadn't thought that far ahead, but automatically said, "The Adams."

Bob knew what I meant: not the original down-wing dry fly invented by Len Halliday in Michigan in 1922 and named after his friend Charles Adams, but the earliest variation of the pattern that most fishermen now think of as the classic Adams: the Catskill-style, upright-winged version that, for a few generations back when things were simpler, was everyone's favorite dry fly.

As anyone who's ever written about this pattern has pointed out, the Adams is custom made for the generalist. By being drab, buggy, and nondescript it looks a little like everything without looking like anything in particular, and its barred grizzly wings and mixed brown and grizzly hackle suggest motion the same way a canary-yellow Ferrari looks like it's going 97 miles an hour even when it's parked at the curb.

Fishermen sometimes use the pattern to invoke largely undisturbed streams where the trout are wild and eager, as in, "It's the kind of creek where you can clean up on nothing but an Adams."

Nonfishermen say of the Adams, "Jeez, that looks just like a real bug," even though it really doesn't if you look at it objectively. But then maybe it does, since trout have been falling for these flies more or less dependably for going on a hundred years now. Who knows what trout think anyway?

I want to say I caught my first trout on an Adams. I can't actually swear to that, but in the way of all apocryphal fishing stories, it at least *sounds* true. I do know that for a long time the backbone of my meager fly selection consisted of Adamses in four or five sizes. That was probably because every fly-fishing writer of that era put the Adams at the top of the list of the five fly patterns every trout fisherman should carry. The other four were usually the Elk Hair Caddis, the Gold-ribbed Hares Ear, the Muddler Minnow, and the Black Woolly Bugger. As I said: simpler times.

This was before I started tying my own flies, so there was the added advantage that anyplace that sold trout flies was bound to carry the Adams. My late father once told me to stay away from weird rifle calibers—"Never own a gun you can't buy bullets for at any hardware store" he said—and that seemed like sound advice for

I think this explosion of new fly patterns was caused partly by the
[gro]wing popularity of fly-fishing—which increased competition on
[the]water—and partly by catch-and-release fishing—which is a use-
[management tool that had the unintended consequence of mak-
[ing t]he trout smarter. And it was probably helped along by the entry
[of a]whole new generation of fly-fishers who appreciated the sport's
[main]ly British, self-consciously classy traditions, but weren't neces-
[sarily] enslaved by them.

[W]hen I first fished the Cheesman Canyon stretch of the South
[Platte] River in Colorado, an Adams in a size 18 would still get you
[through] the spring and fall Blue-wing Olive hatches. But then in the
[late 19]70s, when the canyon became the state's first ever catch-and-
[release] area, hatch-matching fishermen began inadvertently training
[trout t]o be more suspicious of artificial flies. An Adams would [work]
[still w]ork most days, but those in the know started backing it up with
[B]lue Quills and Blue-wing Olives for picky fish in slower water.
[When th]ose flies started to be greeted with skepticism by trout that
[had bee]n caught on them before, they were further backed up by
[paradun]es, No-hackles, Compara-duns, assorted cripples and still-
[born, al]l manner of floating nymphs and emergers, plus a whole
[lot of o]ther bright ideas that never got so far as being named. It
[was p]ossible to carry a dozen fly patterns for a single hatch, and

[A frien]d said he thought that in the search for efficiency we'd lost
[the pur]ity of the sport. He vowed to fish an entire season with
[only] the flies of his youth: the Royal Coachmen, Gray-hackle
[Yellows a]nd Renegades that had gotten him by just fine as a boy in
[Ohio. I]n November of that year he said he was glad to have got-
[ten it out of] his system.

[There w]ere the usual growing pains. The first parachute dry flies
[I saw w]ere tied on special hooks with steel posts sticking off

fly patterns, too. God help you if your favorite dry fly was the Rat-
faced McDougal and you couldn't tie your own.

When I did start tying my own flies, the Adams was one of the
first patterns I learned. (The mixed hackles gave me fits until a friend
told me to try wrapping them one at a time instead of together.) And
when I decided to keep a small flock of chickens for eggs, meat, and
feathers, I chose barred Plymouth rocks, the birds grizzle hackle
comes from. I wasn't so naive as to think I could raise high-quality,
genetically engineered dry fly hackle in the old tool shed behind the
house, but at least when I killed pullets I'd not only get free-range
frying chickens, but good Adams wing feathers.

I lived out in the country where I could let my little flock forage
freely, but at around that same time a woman I knew got a ticket
for illegally keeping chickens inside the town limits. Instead of just
paying the fine she went to court and when her case was called she
said, "Your Honor, I'm afraid I've run 'a fowl' of the law." It was a
risky move, but the judge had a sense of humor and she got off easy.
Not long after that the statute was changed to allow people to keep
chickens in town as long as they penned them up so they wouldn't
peck holes in their neighbors' heirloom tomatoes. The godawful predawn caterwauling of roosters fell under a separate noise ordinance.

For a few years after that chickens multiplied like rabbits. This
was in the early days of the natural food movement, and before people learned how much trouble they could be, backyard chickens became such a fad that our local square dance band began calling itself
"Poultry in Motion."

Learning to tie my own flies seemed like a good idea at the time
and still does, but it didn't exactly go as planned. For one thing, I
expected to save money. After all, I was paying as much as 65 cents
apiece for flies that consisted of nothing more than a three-cent
hook, a few chicken feathers, and a pinch of fur. But then the initial

investment in tools and materials (the cheapest I could find, naturally) plus a copy of *Western Trout Fly Tying Manual* by Jack Dennis was more than I expected and I still didn't have a single fly to show for it. Somehow I hadn't factored in the learning curve. And then, sometime later, there was a second wave of investment after my friend and mentor, A. K. Best, told me that the most I'd ever be able to do with dull scissors and mediocre materials would be to tie mediocre flies. It was a long time (if ever) before I started saving money, but my tying improved with practice and there was a fascination with the process and a sense of self-reliance I liked, so it didn't really matter.

The trouble with tying your own flies was that there were so many flies to tie. I want to believe in a golden age when there were just a few classic patterns to choose from—the Adams, Quill Gordon, March Brown, Blue Dun, and so on—but that was never true in my lifetime. In 1950 J. Edson Leonard published a book called *Flies* that cataloged the dressings for 2,200 fly patterns. All the familiar names were there, including the Adams and the Female Adams with its little yellow egg sack (although not the palmer-hackled Delaware Adams or the Adams Irresistible), but most were flies I'd never heard of before or since. I wonder what kind of look you'd get if you walked into a fly shop today and asked for a Red Heckum or a Welshman's Button.

But even as Leonard was compiling his list of existing patterns— and padding his numbers by unearthing the most obscure flies imaginable—books were being published by idiosyncratic fly tiers who were out to reinvent the wheel. The first one that made an impression on me was *A Modern Dry Fly Code*, by Vincent Marinaro, the book that introduced the Thorax Dun. The so-called Thorax Duns you see now are just collar-hackled dry flies with the hackle trimmed off on the bottom, but the originals had oversize teal flank

wings painstakingly shaped with rocker-style wi
burners hadn't been invented yet) and a kind of fig
hackle that I struggled with, but never got the har
were the precursors of parachute flies, but they
cause they were too hard to tie.

Later there were books by Caucci and Nasta
ards, Gary Lafontaine, Randall Kaufmann, Ch
Best, Ken Iwamasa, Rene Harrop, and too ma
all with their own peculiar ideas about flies.
books once told me he loved to print books
cause there was a small but dependable read
automatically buy every new title, sight unse

Once, the goal of fly tiers had been to
copies of existing patterns following reci
inviolable. But then, almost overnight,
tion as the benchmark and the new ide
unique enough to put your name on an
fame. (It's little enough to ask and a lot
life-threatening with a GoPro strapped
families of flies started coming out ev
with the same expectation that you'd
trends or be left in the dust by the co

Some new patterns were just cu
within a few weeks of publication.
for a while. Some developed region
caught on elsewhere. The most suc
alized fly *types* that were tweaked
until, in some cases, their origins

And, it must be said, some fi
tinkered with them as they saw
caught fish in happy anonymity.

gro
the
ful
ing
of a
vagu
sarily
W
Platte
by on
mid-1
release
the tro
still pas
a few B
When t
had bee
Parachu
borns, a
slew of o
became p
some did.
A frien
the simpli
nothing bu
peacocks, a
the 1950s.
ten it out of
There w
I ever saw

the top of the hook shanks. That made the hackle easy to wind, but added weight to the hooks and ruined their balance so that the flies floated on their sides or upside down. It wasn't until smarter tiers than me realized you didn't need rebar to wrap the hackles that I bought into parachutes. Later I became a true believer when my friend Ed Engle showed me how to tie off the thread under the hackle instead of behind the eye, an operation that, as far as I can see, takes three hands.

And people kept reinventing extended body flies. Every few seasons there was a new brainstorm about how to construct the abdomens on mayfly patterns, but they all shared the same failing of being time-consuming and labor-intensive to tie, while the trout never seemed to think they were anything special. There was even a thing called the Flybody hook on the market with a steel post sticking off the back like the tail of a dog as an armature for the dubbed body. You could tie beautiful mayfly duns on these things, but that rigid steel tail threw off the balance, so the flies didn't float right, and it also tended to act as a lever, pushing the fly out of the mouths of any trout that tried to bite it.

I don't mean to sound superior here. Everything I've mentioned is something I once bought into, learned how to tie, and then tried out on real live fish. I told myself I was field-testing patterns, but my results were never what you'd call definitive. All I really learned is that if you fish any fly long and hard enough you'll catch a few trout on it. Maybe the real challenge would be to come up with a pattern that fish *won't* bite.

And of course more often than not, trying out new and different patterns meant buying new hooks, materials, tools, and books, or, later, instructional videotapes, all of which kept the day when I'd start saving money by tying my own flies perpetually out in front of me like a carrot on a stick.

I feel that I've stayed more or less abreast of the newest fly patterns, not to mention the sometimes overwrought theories they're based on, but I cling to my old ways and several times over the last decade or so younger fishermen have peered into my fly boxes and declared them to be "old school." I was never sure what they meant by that, so I decided to take it as a compliment.

I now have a more or less standard repertoire of flies that I depend on for most of my trout fishing, patterns that aren't strictly realistic, but are poetically drab in the provocative style of the Adams. But at the same time I've always been a sucker for specialized regional patterns—the more obscure the better—and I worry enough about not having the right fly on unfamiliar water to be one of those gullible tourists fly shop owners love to see walking through the door. But then out on the stream I usually pay more attention to my cast and drift than to what I've tied on. If I catch more fish than I used to—and I'm not sure I do—that would be the main reason.

Of course I do make an exception for the Royal Wulff, with its big white calf tail wings and its green and red body that reminds me of a Christmas ornament. All of us naturalists have a favorite attractor pattern that we consider to be the exception that proves the rule. For that matter, I'm happy to fish fantastically gaudy flies for salmon and steelhead and have been known to fish for bass with deer hair bugs that resemble poisonous rain forest tree frogs, but that's a whole other story.

But I still get nostalgic for the days when I could cram my entire trout fly selection into a single tin box not much bigger than a wallet. It reminds me of a lost innocence that, to be honest, may never have actually existed, even though I sometimes miss it terribly. But at the time—as an ambitious tier and a budding match-the-hatch fisherman—I wanted encyclopedic fly boxes like the ones pictured in books and magazine articles written by experts: row after row of devastatingly realistic flies that looked like the author had wrangled real live insects to stand at attention in neat ranks organized by size. It never occurred to me that those photos were staged and that no real fisherman's boxes were ever that neat.

My own fly boxes always were, and still are, a perpetual mess, with pigtails of leader attached to the eyes of hooks; mashed and unraveling flies that should be thrown away, but may still be good enough to fish in a pinch; odds and ends that I picked up on trips and didn't fish, but that still look promising; dry flies with droppers still attached; flies put away in the wrong boxes where I'll never find them again; experiments that didn't pan out, or at least haven't panned out yet; flies that were given to me by friends and helpful strangers that I'll never fish, but somehow can't discard, and so on. As lean and efficient as I aspire to be as a fisherman, I'm often short of the flies I use and well stocked on the ones I don't. (And come to think of it, why am I carrying flies I don't use?)

The Adams is one of those flies I don't fish very often, but that has special status as a pattern I wouldn't be without under any circumstances. A size 14 Adams is still a fine search pattern on the small mountain and foothills creeks I like so much: fast-flowing freestone streams where, as a friend once said, "All that shit from the old fishing books still works."

And there are those odd days when a persnickety tailwater rainbow that has inspected and rejected my best quill-bodied, trailing shuck parachutes and trapped-wing floating emergers will woof a size 20 Adams without a moment's hesitation. No telling why. Maybe trout appreciate the Adams as metaphor. Or maybe I'm somehow able to telegraph my own sentimentality down line and leader and into the fly itself, making it irresistible. Then again, since if you ask for an Adams now you'll probably get the ubiquitous parachute version, there's a fair chance that the trout in question has never seen the authentic article before and so the original voodoo still works.

Sometimes I think it can't be a coincidence that my fly boxes have multiplied and filled with specialized patterns at about the same rate that my life has gotten cluttered with time-consuming complications and electronic noise, while the Adams recalls a time of letters instead of emails, newspapers instead of the Internet, and rotary-dial telephones permanently attached to walls. So where it was once nothing special to catch a trout on an Adams, it now feels delightfully unsophisticated, like giving up your dreams of stardom to go into the family plumbing business or marrying your high school sweetheart.

When you tie your own flies you'll eventually develop a particular sense of how they should look and among other things I want my Adams wings to be made of the rounded, finely marked feathers from barred Plymouth rock hen or pullet capes, but good ones can be hard to find. Most grizzly wing feathers are too narrow and the barring on many of the fatter ones isn't fine enough for small flies. But luckily I've been squirreling away certain fly-tying materials for years and have, among other things, a small stack of primo grizzly pullet capes stashed in a sweater box along with a handful of mothballs.

I started pack-ratting on the advice of Mike Lawson, who once said that if you find a fly-tying material you can't live without, you should go ahead and get yourself a lifetime supply because sooner or later it'll get too expensive or become unavailable. That was an offhanded comment made decades ago, but it begged a question I've been pondering ever since: When it's all said and done, what can't I live without?

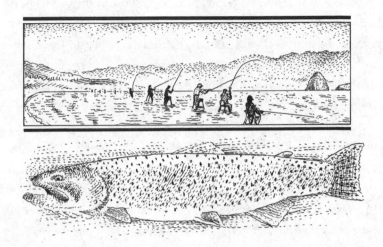

16.

PYRAMID LAKE

We're at an establishment called Crosby's getting deep-fried burritos for breakfast. It's early morning and the place is full of fishermen. Many exhibit the easy familiarity of locals, greeting everyone by name, while others are just as evidently tourists, including some who seem to have settled for gas station coffee when they really wanted a half-caff caramel macchiato. I'm a tourist myself, but maybe less obvious than some. For one thing, I've always been one of those guys who could put on a coat and tie and still be mistaken for the janitor. For another, I'm with Rob Hagerty, the kind of boisterous local guide who knows everyone and whose company bestows some credibility.

Crosby's constitutes the entire business district of the reservation town of Sutcliffe, Nevada, population 253. Short of driving to Reno, this is where you go to buy gas, groceries, fishing licenses, tackle, beer, coffee, and food, and it's conveniently attached to the kind of country/western bar where the impact tremors from the jukebox register in the gravy on your chicken fried steak. You can also play a slot machine here, take a shower, do a load of laundry, store your boat or RV behind a chain link fence, and rent either a small cabin or a trailer with a hookup. ("That's a 'hookup,' not a 'hooker,'" they'll say with a straight face.)

I was staying on the beach out at Pyramid Lake in a borrowed fifth wheel with a working heater and lights and gallon jugs of water for brewing coffee and judiciously flushing the toilet—usually in that order. The view out my front door was stunning in the monotone way of a desert landscape in late winter and the heater came in handy since in March the days can be chilly and the nights downright cold. This thing was parked at a place called Windless Bay, where the wind howled every night, rocking the trailer on its springs like a big cradle.

A few months earlier Rob had invited me to Nevada to fish for Lahontan cutthroats, which would be a new one for me. I'd caught seven of the fourteen surviving subspecies of cutthroat trout and was intrigued by the idea of adding another one to my life list, but that's not to say this was part of a quest to bag them all. I don't have the patience or the emotional stamina for quests, and anyway that had been done before by at least two writers I know of who'd published well-written books about their exploits. In *Cutthroat: A Journey Through the American West*, Michael Graybrook talked about the high elevation sucking the air from his lungs "like a straw at the bottom of an empty glass" and hail falling on his tent "like gravel poured from the sky." In *Many Rivers to Cross*, M. R. Montgomery simply said, "Any time the trout are hard to catch, you are not in the real west."

The cutthroats in Pyramid Lake now are the original strain once removed. The native fish were lost early in the twentieth century for the usual thoughtless reasons: overfishing—both sport and commercial—plus dewatering and dams on the Truckee River that prevented spawning. In retrospect, it's as if people were *trying* to wipe out the fish, although I'm sure they were as surprised as anyone when it actually happened.

But although Pyramid Lake is still a large body of water at 125,000 acres, it's just a remnant of Lahontan Lake, an inland sea that was once bigger than Lake Ontario. When those prehistoric waters receded at the end of the Pleistocene they stranded isolated populations of Lahontan cutthroats around the region that were later collected, raised in hatcheries, and replanted in Pyramid Lake. Those fish—known as the Pilot Peak strain—had been segregated for so long that their genetics may have no longer been a precise match to the original Pyramid Lake fish, but they were the best available version and are good enough for all but the pickiest connoisseurs. In an imperfect world where two subspecies of cutthroat have already gone extinct and others may soon follow, they constitute an environmental victory.

The lake was crowded in the third week of March. Six weeks earlier flash flooding had washed out roads and bridges, and the Paiute Tribe had closed the lake in the middle of fishing season. Pyramid Lake sits in the Nevada desert and it's in a bowl formed by four mountain ranges that concentrate the heat like a Dutch oven, so there's no fishing during the hot months when shallow-water temperatures reach or exceed the trout's upper avoidance level and the fish retreat to the depths where they'd be out of range of anything short of downriggers anyway.

I'd given up on the trip when Rob called to say that a small part of the lake had reopened—about 30 percent of what you can normally fish—so I booked a flight and hurried out. I didn't foresee that everyone else who'd been champing at the bit would do the same and that we'd all be squeezed together into a relatively short stretch of shoreline. It wasn't the first time eagerness has clouded my judgment.

A crowd of fishermen looks different here than it does in most other places because of the local custom of fishing from atop ladders. The inherent problem is that the fish will often cruise the drop-off shelf that, depending on the water level, can be a long reach for a wading fisherman with limited back-cast room.

The original solution was to wade out as deep as possible, sink a milk crate, and then step up on it to cast. It was better than nothing and did keep your back cast up a little, but there wasn't much room to stand, it only gave you an extra eleven inches, and the crates would sometimes settle so deeply into the soft bottom that they couldn't be retrieved. But it wasn't long before some anonymous local genius realized the obvious and began fishing from a stepladder. This was close to perfect: climbing to the next-to-last rung of a six-foot ladder would nearly double your elevation and you could lean into the step above like the casting brace in a drift boat.

Now, of course, there are actual fishing ladders: utility stepladders that are tricked out with a handle and wheels for dragging, rod and net holders, a fold-out casting platform, and a boat seat. Some fishermen cast from the sitting position, others stand, and still others cast from their feet and then take a seat to watch the dead drift of their Thingamabobbers. The first time I climbed up on one of these things the whole operation felt a little too vertiginous for my taste, but I quickly got used to it and eventually began to feel mildly regal, like a nineteenth-century English sahib hunting tigers from the back of an elephant.

We started at Pelican Point, where Rob's trailer was parked along with several other fifth wheels and dozens of pickups and SUVs. This was the most popular beach currently open and the long line of ladders stretching along the bank gave it the feel of a large construction site. We found a gap in the line, planted a ladder in waist-deep water, and I climbed aboard and started casting with the usual rig: a brace of large bead-head midge pupae suspended four or five feet below an orange bobber on an eight-pound tippet.

I'm told that on days when the fish are more active the drop-off is sometimes marked by the backs of rolling trout and when the light is better you can see the color change in the water that marks the shelf. But the fish *weren't* very active—for reasons we'd wonder about over the next week—and the day was cloudy and chilly with the kind of flat, gray light that left an unreadable sheen on the surface. Still, the drop-off was clearly delineated by a line of orange and chartreuse bobbers stretching two hundred yards north and south—with a gap for the boat ramp—so it was easy enough to measure my cast, take a seat, and wait.

I'm not a fan of what I think of as combat fishing, but this wasn't combative. For one thing, instead of being pointedly ignored, as often happens in crowds, I got neighborly nods and waves from the fishermen closest to me as I mounted up. And in the course of things I learned that a flubbed cast or a missed strike might draw some good-natured hooting, while landing a fish would elicit a congratulatory whoop or a 1960s-style clenched fist salute—all from people who, like me, would much rather have had this beach to themselves.

There's an unstated but specific etiquette here that keeps things civilized. Cast only to your own personal space—an elongated, pie-shaped wedge of water right in front of you—and don't squeeze your ladder in too close to your nearest neighbors. If you leave for any length of time, you're expected to take your ladder with you to make room for someone else, but it's permissible to leave it as a place holder during short errands the way you'd leave your jacket on the back of your chair for a trip to a restaurant bathroom. It's not complicated and a local guide later told me the whole thing is governed by the single, all-encompassing rule: "no assholes allowed."

A few hours later I'd landed my first two Lahontan cutthroats— one a fat 18-incher—blown a strike while daydreaming, and come to terms with what I'd first considered a mob scene. I hadn't changed my mind about fishing in a crowd, but I'd decided that if I have to do it, this is the kind of crowd I want.

The draw here for most isn't so much the rare subspecies of cutthroats as their occasional size. Most of the fish caught are on the high end of normal—a keeper is between 17 and 20 inches long or over 24 inches—but every now and then enormous fish weighing 20 pounds or more are landed. This doesn't happen every day and when it does it's likely to make the local newspaper, but it's what the lake is known for. The first thing you notice when you walk into Crosby's are all the mounts of large fish—including a replica of the official world record Lahontan, a 41-pounder caught in 1925—and the south wall is papered with snapshots of big cutthroats, none smaller than about 15 pounds.

These are big trout by anyone's standards, but there are reliable albeit unofficial reports from the old days of cutthroats weighing as much as 60 pounds. That's a number I had to stop and think about. We're talking about cutthroat trout the size of a respectable tarpon or a world-class Atlantic salmon living in a landlocked desert lake in the American West. There was no mention of how those enormous trout were caught, but I can almost guarantee you it wasn't on a size 12 midge pattern fished on a fly rod.

Trophy fisheries naturally attract head hunters, but the whole size business can also get under the skin of otherwise normal fishermen enough to make the perfect enemy of the good and cause them to be mildly disappointed by what would normally be an impressive cut-throat. I landed at least some fish every day except one and my big-gest was a little over 22 inches long, a thick male with a pre-spawning flush of rosy pink on his broad flanks. He was handsome enough that I took a picture of him to show friends back home, but at the time Rob just said something like, "Let's see if we can get you a big one." I thought, *Where I come from, that is a big one*, but I didn't say any-thing. Rob was just fulfilling his mandate as a trophy guide whose clients expect him to produce on demand like a professional athlete, only at a lower pay grade; he wasn't really trying to spoil it for me.

But I'm not here to tell anyone what their attitude about fishing should be. Way back in high school I was often told that my attitude was unacceptable and once I even blurted out what I was thinking: that they could tell me what to do, but my attitude was my own and none of their business. I still believe that, even after the stern lecture from the principal about the probable bleakness of my future "with an attitude like that."

And understand, too, that I'd have been delighted to catch a 20-pound cutthroat—or at least hook one and try my best to land it—and pose for one of those hero shots where you shove the fish's face into a wide-angle lens to make it look even bigger than it actually is. It's just that I was at peace with how unlikely that was and couldn't bring myself to turn up my nose at "smaller" cutthroats between 18 and 22 inches when back home a 10-incher will make your day.

I did see two good fish landed that week. One was around 10 pounds, the other more like 12; both impressive double-digit cut-throats, though probably not quite big enough to make the wall at Crosby's.

By then we'd moved to a less crowded beach where only five or six other fishermen were spread out over a hundred yards of shoreline. This was the coldest, windiest day of the week and my slowest day of fishing. Everyone had long since agreed that the fishing was off, but we still hadn't figured out why and never would. The water was still slightly off color from the flood, but not enough to make a difference. The fish should have liked the heavy cloud cover; the chilly weather wasn't unusual; and the waves caused by the onshore wind were the kind that stir small organisms off the bottom that attract bait fish that in turn attract big trout. Or so the theory goes.

But the fishing was off anyway and I wasn't surprised. Floods shake things up—even if it's not always clear how—and I've always had the uncanny ability to show up for the worst week of fishing anyone has seen in five years. Like most savants with an instinctive skill, I have no idea how I do this; it just comes naturally.

I'd been casting a streamer from my ladder, standing for the long punch into the headwind and then sitting to make my erratic retrieve. I was fishing a streamer I'd gotten from a local fisherman; I'd located the drop-off by feeling for the tick as the deeply sunken fly bumped the soft, sandy lip of the shallows, and with extra room around me I could cast to a wider wedge and cover more water. I felt like I had this wired except for the fact that I hadn't had a touch all morning.

Across the water to the east the barren mountains of the Lake Range seemed to rise right up out of the lake itself looking like the arid Sierra de la Giganta on the Sea of Cortez except for the dusting of fresh snow on their peaks. A mile or so to the north a long point of land stuck out into the water with a plume of steam from a hot spring rising from between rock formations and leaning west with the prevailing wind.

Rob had told me earlier that all that land was off-limits to anyone except tribal members because it was "sacred land." I didn't doubt it for a minute, but I did remember a First Nations man from Canada explaining that the idea of sacredness didn't always translate well between our two cultures. That's because many native people think the whole world and everything in it is sacred, while we Anglos reserve the label for a few specific pieces of real estate and see everything else as a potential site for a strip mine. But they'll use the term to get a point across and in part because, as the man said, "You white guys are suckers for any kind'a spooky Indian shit."

Late in the morning I noticed that a wading fisherman way down the beach to my left was backing out of the water with a bent rod—the first fish I'd seen hooked all day—and a few minutes later a man on a ladder thirty or forty yards to my right also hooked one. It took him long enough to land it that I reeled in to watch the show and when his guide got it in the net it turned out to be the 10-pounder.

He'd been fishing something suspended under a bobber, so I nipped off my streamer and was still rerigging with a brace of midge pupae and a strike indicator when the same guy hooked and landed the 12-pounder. I thought, *Okay, this is it; a pod of big fish has moved in to graze along the drop-off and it's only a matter of time.*

Watching someone land a couple of large trout on what was beginning to look like a blank day makes you envious and hopeful and does wonders for your concentration, but none of that lasts forever. An hour later I was still perched on my ladder. The plume of steam from the hot spring was now almost horizontal as the cold wind picked up and I was wondering how close you'd have to get to the hot spring to feel the warmth. Meanwhile the surface of the lake kept changing from gray to opaque turquoise for no apparent reason.

No more fish had been hooked and the guy who'd landed the two big trout had gone back to his car for lunch, which was starting to seem like a pretty good idea. I was cold, bored, hungry, and fishless, but there was still nowhere else I'd have rather been—something anyone who fishes will understand.

17.

THE WORLD'S GREATEST
TROUT STREAM

Russell Chatham once published an essay called "The World's Great-est Trout Stream," which was a masterpiece of angling misdirection. He was impenetrably vague about the location of the stream, includ-ing not specifying what country it's in (although if you guessed New Zealand I think you'd be right) and referring to the three friends he was fishing with as Larry, Curly, and Moe, so you couldn't even sub-poena eyewitnesses. As the title implies, the place sounds almost too good to be true and at times Chatham seems to be daring his read-ers to believe him. On the other hand, the narrative is so plausible it's hard to imagine that these are imaginary events happening in a made-up place, although of course making fictional incidents and locations seem real is a trick a good writer can pull off.

I not only believe the story for the most part, but I understand the author's dilemma. As a writer, you can't resist telling a good yarn, but as a fisherman you're proprietary about any honey hole you know of and terrified of revealing even some seemingly insignificant detail that could end up spilling the beans. Fishermen are secretive precisely because we've all seen the beans get spilled from time to time and the results were never good.

Over the years, mostly through dumb luck and the kindness of strangers, I've spent time on a precious handful of streams and rivers that struck me while I was there—and for some time afterward—as at least in the running for the world's greatest. What interests me now is why I thought that.

The first time I caught west slope cutthroats was when a guide friend in Canada asked me if I wanted to go with him to scout a river he'd been hearing about but had never fished. So we towed his drift boat over a mountain pass between one province and another, bought nonresident licenses, rented a cheap motel room in a nearby small town, and spent four days doing back-to-back ten-mile floats.

The river through that stretch flowed past a range of the Canadian Rockies that rivaled the Grand Tetons for scenery and it had fishy runs interspersed with rapids that pumped oxygen and aquatic insects into the water like factories on overtime. My memory wants to make every cutthroat trout we caught at least 20 inches long and fat as a piglet, while in fact only some of them were, but more than enough to keep things interesting.

Green Drake mayflies were hatching that week and after we burned through our meager supply of Drake patterns we found that the fish were just as happy with a Royal Wulff, a Humpy, or an

Adams. Any old dry fly in a size 10 or 12 was close enough for those unsophisticated fish. It can't have actually been true, but they acted as if they'd never before seen a fly that wasn't real. But then maybe it *was* true because in forty miles of floating over four days during the height of the season we never saw another boat and spotted only one other fisherman casting a spinning rod from the bank. He smiled and waved in that cordial, Canadian way, apparently delighted to see us.

This became a regular trip for a while and I did notice some changes here and there as time went by, but the last time I went back, eighteen years after that first trip, I found the place being carpet-bombed by the recreation industry. A ski resort had sprung up almost overnight, the cheap motels had been replaced by luxury condos, and the mom-and-pop cafes were now bistros. Fly shops had sprouted like mushrooms and in that forty miles of vacant river we'd floated almost two decades earlier you could now count a hundred drift boats on any given day. The fishing was still good, but the trout had gotten somewhat smaller, there were noticeably fewer of them, and some had begun to refuse even natural insects out of an abundance of caution. At least my guide friend was making a good living.

In retrospect, it's amazing the river held up as long as it did, being right out there in the open where anyone could find it. On the other hand, I did get in on some of the last best years there and that may be the happiest ending this story could have had in the waning seasons of the twentieth century. So maybe I shouldn't complain. Maybe this is just why old fishermen get sentimental.

And there was a small mountain creek somewhere in the American Southwest. This was Rio Grande cutthroat water and it also held big trout, although not as big as that river in Canada because of the small scale and high elevation of the stream. Still, 16-inch cutthroats weren't all that uncommon and that's an astonishing size in this kind of miniature, marginal water.

Those fish were there because the hike into the sweet spot was long and steep and the pristine water above was camouflaged in its lower reaches in such an effective and peculiar way that if I described it I'd risk revealing its location. (I haven't been back there in years, but there's the off chance that this place is still undiscovered by fish hogs.)

When a kindly local led my friend and me in there after extracting a vow of silence, I thought this death march must be a cruel practical joke, but I slogged on in good faith anyway, hoping for the best. At least I was traveling light. By then I'd learned the hard lesson that a good fisherman, like a good cook, can usually get the job done with a few simple utensils, while all the specialized, high-tech gizmos just add weight and take up space. Still, I was about out of breath when we dropped down to the last bench of land and saw the stream fifty yards below us. Even at that range we could see trout rising and I abandoned my plan to stop there and rest for a few minutes.

I'll spare you the blow-by-blow account and just say that the stream was full of fat cutthroats, including some of those 16-inchers. The day was bright and cool, the water was clear, and we could cherry-pick the biggest fish and watch them glide to the surface to eat our dry flies with an innocence that was heartbreaking.

We left while there was still enough daylight for the long but thankfully downhill slog out and on that hike I told the guy who'd led us there that if there was ever any way I could return the favor he should let me know. He said, "Well, now that you mention it . . ." and before he even got the rest out I thought, *Okay, fair enough.*

And there was another stream in Canada. This one also held west slope cutts and it was about the size of that stream in the Southwest, but at a lower altitude and much closer to its confluence with a larger river that took the brunt of the fishing pressure. It wasn't as well hidden, either, but it was roadless, a little on the obscure side, and had

a reputation for being infested with grizzly bears. Both times I fished it I did see some fresh bear sign, but I think its woolly reputation was mostly a ploy by the locals who knew and loved it.

Still, bear stories have a way of getting under your skin and when a blue grouse flushed at my feet on my first day I found myself gasping for breath with an overdose of adrenaline roaring in my ears. But the trout there ranged from 16 to more than 20 inches and they had a soft spot for dry flies, so it seemed worth the emotional wear and tear.

The last I heard, word had leaked out to the extent that there's now a fisherman's trail along the bank and an improvised pullout on the nearest dirt road. The stream still draws good reviews, but the fact that there are reviews at all (even whispered ones among friends) is an ominous sign.

I haven't been back to any of those places in a long time. I could say that life is short and other streams beckon, and that would be true enough, but the fact is I'm afraid to go because the world changes too fast now for sentimental journeys to pan out very often. It usually turns out that the quiet lake you fished as a kid is now buzzing with jet-skis, the old family farm with its bass pond is now a shopping center, and Grandma's house, if it's there at all, has been remodeled into an unrecognizable hipster monstrosity. Your recollections may be warped by the passage of time, but not as badly as time itself warps reality, so it's probably best for your sanity to keep those memories intact.

I couldn't help writing about some of those streams at the time, but I was always careful to avoid mentioning their names or to make up fictitious ones; to move them from one state or province to another; to misidentify Engelmann spruce as ponderosa pine, and sometimes to import identifiable features like lens-shaped pools fed by waterfalls from other streams in order to throw the hounds off the scent. As a literary justification, I made the stories about something other than the exact locations of these waters, like solitude or the importance of keeping secrets. The only tactic I never resorted to was to claim I'd been fishing with the Three Stooges, even though on one occasion that wouldn't have been far off. Did that strategy render me blameless in those cases where the inevitable happened anyway? God, I hope so.

My current thinking is that the world's greatest trout stream may be in a remote corner of northern Canada that's known for the big native brook trout that have lived there undisturbed—except for the odd fisherman—since the last ice age. I started going there in the mid-1990s and since then I've gotten homesick if I stayed away for more than a few seasons in a row. This region is a logistical nightmare to get around in, not to mention getting to in the first place, but I don't know what I'd do without it.

At first I went simply for the size of the brook trout and chose a camp that claimed the average fish caught there weighed five pounds, which would be the brook trout of a lifetime anywhere else I'd fished. I've always prided myself on not being a numbers guy, but on that trip I kept track of every fish my partner and I landed, with the help of the guides who recorded the weight of every brook trout their clients caught. Those numbers were then entered in a log book that had been handed down from one head guide to the next since the camp opened in the 1960s. That week we caught brook trout weighing between three and seven pounds and, sure enough, our average worked out to be just a hair over five pounds.

The policy at that camp was catch and release on brook trout except that clients could kill one fish per trip to mount if they wanted to. That seemed reasonable enough—especially considering how remote this region was—until I begged a look at that old log book, with its early pages brittle and fading, and saw that the weights of the biggest fish had declined over the years by as much as a pound or two. The camp manager told me most people were happy with a hero shot and didn't want to spring for an expensive mount, so very few fish had ever been kept—and there were no fish corpses in the freezer at the end of our week there—but the cumulative effect was still undeniable.

Since then, at a second camp and then at a third where I've become a chronic recidivist (and where the rule has been catch and release since the camp opened), I've caught some eight-pounders—not many, but some—and two that came within a few ounces one way or the other of nine pounds. The first of those fish was verified by a guide and a reliable bystander. The second was caught while I was alone without a scale or a camera and the only proof I have is the permanent set in an old 6-weight bamboo rod. But I'm confident that my educated guess wasn't the product of hysteria. Aside from the one I'd already landed, I'd seen two other nine-pounders caught, so at that point I actually knew what a nine-pound brook trout looked and felt like, which is not something I thought I'd ever be able to say.

If my goal had been to catch the biggest brook trout possible, I'd more or less arrived. Biologists say the brook trout at this far northern end of their ancestral range live longer than most—up to ten years in the wild—and that the waters are so rich in food organisms that their growth rate can average out to a pound a year.

The math you can't help doing is tantalizing, but deceptive. In a dozen trips to this region I've heard second- and third-hand stories (one involving Lee Wulff roll-casting off the pontoon of a floatplane), but I've never spoken to anyone who's seen a double-digit brook trout in the flesh, although I've talked to some who think there must be a few out there somewhere. But for those of us living in the fact-based universe, a nine-pound brook trout constitutes a pinnacle of

171

accomplishment, while a 10-pounder falls somewhere between theoretically possible and mythological.

I fished the world's greatest trout stream on a cool, buggy summer day last year with three friends: a sporting artist, a photojournalist, and the owner of the lodge where we were staying. I won't tell you the name of this stream, but even if I did you wouldn't be able to look it up. When the lodge owner scouted the stream and found fish there, he named it for his own convenience, but it's a name known only to the handful of people who need to know and not one you'll find on any map.

It's hardly a stream at all: just a channel less than a mile long that drains one small, nameless lake into another. There's a wide, dogleg pool at the top end before the stream narrows into something that resembles a mountain creek in the Rockies, only not as steep, running through the kind of thick black spruce woods where you have to watch every back cast. In a region where most running water is accessible in a canoe with an outboard, it's the kind of place that's almost guaranteed to be overlooked.

I won't pointlessly build drama here. Most of the brook trout we caught were between one and two pounds, handsome, chunky fish that were already putting on the girth that would turn those that survived for a few more years into the hump-backed, deep-bellied bruisers that can venture out into bigger water with the hungry pike and lake trout. That doesn't count one shallow nursery pool full of fingerling brookies I found. I didn't spend much time there, but I did let a few baby fish beach-ball my big dry fly with the same delight you feel when playing with a puppy.

During a lunch break we agreed that this little body of water was a creek fisher's wet dream, the kind of place you wouldn't even tell your mother about. It had native trout way out of proportion to their small water and flowed through surroundings that couldn't be wilder, lonelier, or more remote. And it was all enhanced by that tickle at the back of your mind that comes from being dropped off at the nearest lake by a floatplane that's supposed to be back to pick you up that evening—barring something unforeseen like engine trouble, a change in the weather, or some other mishap. You don't think about it constantly, but when you finally hear the drone of that big radial engine in the distance, you realize you'd been unconsciously on the edge of your chair all day.

Furthermore, this stream is in a region so difficult, time-consuming, and expensive to reach that even the few who go to the trouble are looking for trophy-size fish and this little creek is so mediocre by local standards that a head-hunter wouldn't think twice about it, so its secret could be safe for a hundred years. Even in your worst dystopian nightmares it's doubtful it'll ever get crowded or fished out.

I was the first to make it down to within sight of the next lake. I caught a somewhat larger brook trout in the last plunge pool— maybe two and a half pounds—and below that the stream slowed, widened, and deepened with the main current hugging the far bank in the shade of overhanging alders. It was the kind of water I'd learned to recognize, so I swapped out my size 10 Parachute Wulff for a size 6 orange Bomber and skated up first a four- and then a five-pound brook trout. These probably weren't creek fish, but big boys that had worked their way up from the lake below to feed—not that it mattered.

Downstream the creek got wider and deeper yet and the current finally stalled out just beyond casting range in the next lake. That was also recognizable. In fact, it was in a spot very much like this that, only days earlier, the photojournalist had landed an eight-pound brook trout as thick and solid as a side of ribs.

I stared at this pristine meat bucket for a while, picking out places where I thought fish might be. Then I reeled in and found a comfortable place to sit. Maybe I was tired, maybe I was done, or maybe I'd just reached that point in a good day of fishing that must be honored by a moment of silence. Anyway, I thought I'd just enjoy the view of this nameless stream inlet somewhere in Canada and wait for my three friends, Larry, Curly, and Moe.

18.

A GOOD YEAR FOR MUSKIES

I came home from my last scheduled fishing trip of the season in October with an ache in my casting elbow that I recognized as tendonitis. This had happened twice before: once in the same elbow when I tried to keep a fat bass out of a weed bed in Texas and once in the wrist when I mistakenly thought a big silver salmon in Alaska was ready to be beached. Who knew fly-fishing could be so dangerous?

This time the story doesn't sound so heroic. The elbow was just sore after a day of musky fishing on the Wisconsin River and it not only stayed sore, but got worse over the next two weeks. It was late in a long fishing season and this felt less like a traumatic injury and more like what my mechanic would call "excessive wear on a high-mileage part."

I knew two things from experience: that however tempting it was to wait it out, it wouldn't go away on its own and that in fact the longer I ignored it the worse it would get. I snuck out one last time for the end of the Blue-wing Olive hatch on a nearby river, but casting even a light 4-weight rod made me wince and striping in an eight-inch trout actually hurt.

So now I'm wearing an elbow brace, undergoing a course of dry-needling (a kind of gringo acupuncture), slathering on arnica ointment, icing the tendon, and so on. And it's been suggested that I not swing a hammer, split wood, or cast a fly rod pending further notice. As a childhood fan of two-fisted John Wayne movies I want to shrug this off as nothing but a flesh wound, while in weak moments I feel like a bird with a broken wing, but either way sympathy is scarce. Even fishing friends aren't all that sure they feel sorry for me and when non-anglers learn that I hurt myself by fishing too much, they'll say, "Oh, you poor baby!" without even trying to suppress their sarcasm.

Usually when I'm casting big flies for muskies I can manufacture a passable two-handed water haul that plops the fly tight to the bank while preserving my elbow through the countless casts they say it takes to hook one of these things. Apparently I'm not the only one who does it this way because a prototype musky rod I tried out this fall had a long extended bottom grip reminiscent of a Spey rod for extra leverage on a two-handed haul. But although the long grip was as comfortably ergonomic as an ax handle, the rod itself didn't have the backbone to lob a fly with the aerodynamics of a wet gym sock. Further research is indicated.

Almost all of the large musky flies I've used were tied with layers of spun bucktail, each overlapping the last like palm fronds on a thatched roof, and highlighted with saddle hackle and tinsel. These flies can be up to a foot long, so naturally the longest hair is best for the job, but it's so hard to find that one musky guide I met who started a side business wholesaling bucktails with the ulterior motive of pawing through thousands of them and high-grading the best for his own flies. These patterns have great body and action in the water, but once they're wet they're so heavy in the air that false casting them quickly becomes futile, hence the water haul.

But that day on the Wisconsin our guide, Abe, thought we should hang farther off the bank than I'm used to, forcing me into an athletic double haul with a heavy rod and a big waterlogged fly that, over eight or nine hours, gradually blew out my elbow. In my fishing fantasies the one thing I never imagine myself doing is wearing out, but it happens, and something in my American male upbringing precludes me from ever being the first to say, "I gotta rest for a while."

At first I didn't see the necessity of those long casts because muskies aren't known to be spooky, but I reminded myself that if you don't think your guide knows more about the river than you do, you shouldn't have hired him. As it turned out, my partner and I moved five fish that day, which constitutes a pretty good session of musky fishing. It's just that those fish were in a mood, charging and boiling at our flies, but not eating and not coming back for another look at subsequent casts.

It was those explosive short strikes that kept me casting even though my elbow had begun to ache dangerously. I'd had this same sense of impending drama years before on a river in British Columbia where I was happily catching west slope cutthroats until a yard-long bull trout ate a 15-incher off my leader ten feet from the boat. I asked, "What the fuck was that?" and the angling possibilities abruptly expanded. I found that I couldn't be happy again until I caught one of those big fish—and when I did, it turned out that one wasn't enough.

Of course gaining purchase on unfamiliar tackle and the psychology of an unfamiliar fish is time-consuming. A lifetime of fishing gives you a frame of reference, but taken together the fine points are still obscure enough to make you a beginner all over again. To hear some fishermen tell it, it's possible to be an expert on everything that swims, but among us mere mortals there may only be room in a lifetime to fully come to terms with a single species, while everything else remains exotic.

So it's not unusual for the entire first trip to be more or less a bust, fish-wise, with the saving grace that you begin to see how things are. With muskies, more can go wrong than right—especially on the strike—and there are so few strikes that it takes forever to learn from your mistakes. Never mind that they're all mistakes you'd been warned about. If you don't get excited enough to blow a chance due to nerves, why even bother? At the end of a trip like that you can quote Thomas McGuane, who once said "Fishing isn't really about success," but if that enlightened sentiment were true we wouldn't howl obscenities at a missed fish.

What rattles your composure with muskies is their size. A 40-inch musky is only a keeper, while serious bragging rights begin at 50 inches and go up incrementally from there. To put that in context, the Fresh Water Fishing Hall of Fame in Wisconsin lists the world record musky as a 60¼-inch fish weighing 69 pounds, 11 ounces, caught by Louis Spray in 1949. Meanwhile, the International Game Fish Association, headquartered in Florida, awards the record to another 60¼-inch fish weighing 67 pounds, 8 ounces that was caught by Cal Johnson in the same year as Spray's fish. I was only three years old in 1949, but it was a good year for muskies.

As the largest members of the pike family and the apex predators in their environment, muskies have the personalities of grizzly bears. They're fully capable of the violence they're famous for, but are just as likely to be lazy, uninterested, or merely curious. Follows are more common than strikes and it's never clear what the fish has in mind, since biologists say their usual MO is to lurk motionlessly, then curl into an S shape and strike like a snake. Sometimes there'll be an ominous wake behind a fly that stops your heart, but comes to nothing. Or maybe you'll glimpse a long shadow in the water trailing your streamer, although more often you'll see nothing at all.

That's why you figure-8 the fly at the boat at the end of every retrieve: to induce a strike from an unseen following musky that, 99 casts out of a hundred, isn't there. You do it anyway. The biggest musky I'd caught so far took the fly more or less at my feet and my first indication that the fish was there was when my line came tight. It was broad daylight, the water was less than four feet deep—tannin stained, but clear—and the fish was 47 inches long. How did I not see it?

I've done almost all of my musky fishing on the Chippewa and Flambeau drainages in Wisconsin on the annual trips my friend Bob White puts together to coincide with the Corn Moon in September. That one day on the Wisconsin River where I wrecked my elbow was an outlier. Bob and I and our photographer friend Mike Dvorak were doing a three-day seminar on art, photography, and writing at a museum in Wausau, after which we planned to slip in some late-season trout fishing.

But then the Saturday event Mike and I were scheduled for was canceled for some reason, so we snuck out with Abe to do a float for muskies. Bob couldn't come because he was doing a daylong painting demonstration across the hall from the gallery where his paintings were hung, but he didn't seem at all jealous. He wished us luck and waved, smiling, as we drove off with our guide. That night all he'd say was, "Painting in public is flypaper for weirdos."

For his annual musky trips, Bob assembles the kind of patient local guides who can teach you how to fish for these critters if you give them the raw material to work with. That would be a passable cast, some basic stream-craft, the ability to follow instructions, realistic expectations, and the willingness to dedicate enough time for it all to sink in. In the case of a recalcitrant predator, "time" can mean multiple trips during which you pick up lessons from the guides and just generally begin to sort things out.

A guide named Brad Bowen rowed a boat so small and light it could be car-topped and so narrow the oarlocks were on outriggers. On the water it felt more like a canoe than a rowboat and there were no casting braces, so it seemed wise to take a seat through the riffles. Brad was a fly changer, giving each pattern no more than an hour in the water before switching to something completely different. Once, after staring into his fly box for a long time with his face hidden by the brim of a shapeless straw hat, he handed me a small, frog-like contraption with protruding eyeballs and legs that kicked and dangled. This little thing allowed for an easy conventional cast with a 10-weight rod, although it wasn't what I picture as a musky fly. But then I thought, once again, *Trust you guide. Maybe you're about to learn something new about muskies.*

I still had that fly on when we spotted a large boil in a backwater and eased in to see if it was a musky. It turned out to be a family of river otters chasing something in the shallows and I was just about to comment on how adorable otters were when the two kits crawled out and huddled together on a log, obviously terrified, while the adults came at the boat, snarling, spitting, and baring their teeth. We retreated to the main current and fled downstream, each silently wondering what it would be like to have a pair of angry, 25-pound otters in the boat. At the next bank I changed out the weird little frog for a streamer.

Dan Boggs is all smiles and banter, and his fly choices, like

Brad's, seem somehow keyed to the mood of the moment. Sometimes his hand will hover indecisively over the ranks of flies for sixty full seconds before he plucks something out as if inspiration had finally struck. Other times he'll turn his briefcase-size fly box in your direction and ask, "Anything look good?"

One day he handed me a long, trim streamer tied in black and white with silver tinsel. He called it "Skelator" and said it was inspired by the Halloween costume worn by a woman he met in a bar. "She was tall and thin," he said, as if that explained everything.

Dan knows more jokes than anyone I've ever met and he's not shy about telling them. Most aren't what you'd call good jokes— they're more the kind that elicit a groan and a smile, but a smile nonetheless. He'll trot out a string of them, often related by theme, whenever the conversation flags and silence threatens to overtake the proceedings. Dan believes that once you have the basics down— the cast, the strip, the figure 8, and, when and if the time comes, the vicious and repeated strip strike—the rest is just a matter of keeping the fly in the water. That can begin to seem like drudgery, so when he's guiding for muskies he sees his main job as one of making the time pass pleasantly. At the takeout it's possible to feel like you've just spent a day in a boat with Buddy Hackett.

I learned my preference for using the largest possible musky flies from Luke Swanson. I don't remember ever seeing a pattern in his box that wasn't bigger than most of the trout I catch and realistically drab; there are none of those gaudy, parti-colored numbers that some musky wonks say catch more fishermen than fish. Luke is the youngest of the guides Bob brings in every year for the musky trip— he's in his early twenties—and he's fishy, that dumbfoundingly elusive quality that I think has something to do with a peculiar kind of alertness that you probably have to be born with. He'll spend most of a day rowing, but his boat is fitted with an outboard so he can motor back upstream for a second pass at a promising bank or fish late and then make time down to the takeout at the end of the day.

I was in Luke's boat last year when I landed that 47-inch musky. Forty-seven and a fourth, actually. Luke is a stickler for fractions of an inch and refuses to fudge, even if fudging would nudge a fish up to that arbitrary but venerable 50-inch mark. He believes that muskies like to grab their prey sideways so they get a firmer bite with their wide, bristling jaws. That's why you want to yank hard enough on each strip of your retrieve that the uneven face of the fly combined with the weight of the wire leader cocks the fly sideways in the water. Luke has gone so far as to film live suckers used as musky bait with a GoPro and has footage of muskies nudging suckers from behind until they turn to the side before they'll strike.

This year I went out again with Luke and my friend Dan Frasier. We moved one fish first thing that morning just upstream of the boat ramp, and then fell into what seemed like a slump but was, in fact, just a normal day of musky fishing. By late afternoon Luke decided to try a fork of the river that's usually too low to be navigable with an outboard, but this year the water was up and he thought we could make it. The year before he was still fishing from a conventional drift boat with an outboard fitted to its transom, but by then he'd upgraded to a large aluminum jet boat with raised, carpeted casting decks fore and aft, a bigger outboard on a power lift, an off-center console, and more electronics than a Stealth fighter. So by keeping one eye on the depth finder he managed to ease us up this leafy, shady fork that reminded me of a medium-size trout stream.

We tried the usual spots: eddies with floating maple leaves, a good-looking creek inlet, and then a drop-off along an undercut grassy bank. My fly was two strips off that grass when a fish took in a savage boil, and when I felt the pull I did what every musky guide I've talked to has said to do: I struck back violently and repeatedly with my line hand with the rod still pointed directly at the fish, and then bent the 12-weight rod nearly double to keep the fish from running and to wear it down quickly. The fish had taken a deceptively plain fly of Luke's that I assume is a secret because when he published a photo of the two of us posing with the fish on social media, he Photoshopped out the fly that was still hanging from the musky's jaw.

It was a beautiful fish—two inches shorter than the big one from the previous year, but considerably heavier: a thick, deep-bellied hunk with the emerald green flanks characteristic of river muskies; a color you can't quite believe when you finally lift one of these things from the water.

This wasn't my first musky, but as a novice and a slow learner, it was the first one I felt I'd landed through something resembling skill. When I tried that idea out on Luke he said, with more surprise in his tone than I'd have liked, "You know, you *did*. You actually did everything right." On those occasions when Luke seems a little cocky, I remind myself that he's no cockier than I was at his age.

We fished on for a while, but it was getting late, so pretty soon we squeezed out of that fork into the main river and motored down toward the boat ramp, thinking we'd stop and give the fish we'd moved that morning one last try before we packed it in.

On the way we overtook Dan Boggs slowly rowing out with two other sports from our group. Luke politely throttled down and we passed at no-wake speed, exchanging quick fishing reports and accepting congratulations. Once we'd idled past, and just before he throttled back up, Luke turned to me and said, "You old guys who still like to row rivers crack me up."

19.

UP IN MICHIGAN

Paul was supposed to pick me up at the airport in Grand Rapids, but while I was still waiting to board my flight at the gate in Denver, he sent the brief text: "Billy will meet you." He meant our mutual friend Bill Bellinger, who was there at baggage claim when I got in.

As we drove north out of town, I asked, "So, where's Paul?"

"He had a doctor's appointment," Bill said, which I understood to be the latest of many such appointments with results that had become all too predictable.

Paul had cancer that had first been misdiagnosed as harmless nodes on his vocal cords, then treated with chemo, radiation, and an operation before it was finally declared inoperable, so from here on out the doctor would have nothing but varying degrees of bad news. When Paul told me about his prognosis I asked what he planned to do and he said, "Well, let's go fishing," hence this trip. But there in the pickup on a bright June day, Bill and I had suddenly run out of things to say, so we drove on in silence for the next few miles.

When we got close to the river we made a stop at Gates Lodge so I could buy a Michigan fishing license. I hadn't intended to get any flies, but after cruising the bins and admiring the sparse, delicate local patterns that made the flies I'd brought from home seem too clunky for the job at hand, I picked out a dozen. Then Bill and I walked down to the river and stared at it for a while: a required ritual on new water.

A little farther down the road we turned onto the unmarked sandy two-track winding through second-growth white pine and spruce that led to the borrowed cabin on the Au Sable River where we'd be staying. Paul's pickup was parked out front and we found him napping on the couch. Lately he'd been tiring out easily, so there were lots of naps.

Much of the next day passed at the kind of sleepwalking pace that would come to characterize this trip. We started with a leisurely late breakfast at the cafe at Gates Lodge. There was an item on the menu called "The Hungover Guide" that came with dry toast and a warm Busch Lite. Bill didn't think it was a joke.

From there we moseyed over to meet Bill's guide friend Jimmy Calvin at his small house in the woods, where we stood around talking about the river, the weather, hatches, and fly patterns: another ritual fishermen perform, not so much to get on the same page as to demonstrate that we'd all been on the same page from the beginning. Eventually we trailered up two of Jimmy's Au Sable riverboats, one for Bill and Paul and the other for Jimmy and me. These are the gracefully long, narrow, flat-bottomed pirogues that were once poled up and down these rivers to deliver supplies to logging camps and then evolved into the signature regional fishing boats that fit their home water with hand-in-glove perfection. Jimmy had several of these boats around the place, on and off trailers and in various states of disrepair, with one lost cause repurposed as a planter full of flowers.

We all understood that at this point Paul only had a few good hours of fishing in him before he got too tired to go on, but our slow pace wasn't entirely in deference to him. This was the best month for dry flies in northern Michigan—by one count, twenty distinct hatches come off in June—but the hatches don't start until late in the day and so the fishermen do the same. When we'd left Gates Lodge in late morning there were still knots of fishermen leaning on trailered boats, smoking, talking, and sipping coffee from Styrofoam cups, in no more of a hurry than we were to get started. It would have been just like Paul to have factored this into the timing of the trip so his deteriorating condition wouldn't inconvenience the rest of us. Also just like him not to have mentioned it.

We put in on the North Fork in late afternoon, planning to hit the evening Brown Drake hatch and spinner fall and make the cabin on the main branch at dark. The day had started out sunny and warm, but soon after we got on the water a low overcast moved in, the air turned cool, and as we poled slowly downriver Brown Drake spinners began to form up in the air above us; just a few at first, and then more until a massive mating swarm of mayflies stretched out downstream like an inverted shadow of the river.

It looked promising, but the conditions required for good fishing are precarious. A gray sky like this could put the spinners on the water earlier than usual and trigger a longer rise than you'd see on a clear evening. A little sprinkle wouldn't matter much one way or the other, while actual rain, depending on how hard it was, when it happened, and how long it lasted, could either knock all the bugs onto the surface of the river at once, causing a massive rise, or drive them back into the trees, canceling the spinner fall. And even if everything worked out right, there was the possibility that the spinner fall would be too good, with so many bugs on the water that the likelihood of a feeding trout picking your little fly out of the crowd would be slim. It could be nothing more than this moment-to-moment uncertainty that attracts us to the sport.

An hour or so into the float we were drifting along looking for trout rising to drake duns when it started to rain, lightly at first, and then hard enough for all of us to stop and shrug into our rain gear. I hadn't noticed until then that the sky had turned from gray to slate and then to nearly black upstream as a squall growling with thunder advanced on us.

Jimmy poled over to a cabin on river right and tied off the boat on an exposed root. The cabin was dark and there were no vehicles in the drive, but Jimmy said, "These people won't mind if we duck in here to get out of the rain." Did he mean to say he knew the people, or just that cabin doors are regularly left unlocked here and that *no one* would mind? I was about to ask when the other boat tucked in behind us and I stopped to give Paul a hand up the bank. I was surprised at how light he felt.

When Jimmy opened the back door to the cabin a large St. Bernard pushed past him, walked over to me, and took my entire left hand in his mouth, not biting down, but holding it tightly enough that I didn't know what would happen if I tried to pull it loose. I could feel the points of teeth and a warm tongue the size of a tennis shoe on my palm. Jimmy called from inside, "Don't worry about him, that's just how he says hello." I looked at the dog and said, "You're a *good* boy" with all the conviction I could muster, at which point he released my hand and wagged his tail.

By the time the owners of the cabin came home—a husband and wife and the wife's brother—we were sitting around their kitchen table, eating potato salad and the brats we'd grilled on their hibachi. They were happy to see Jimmy and didn't seem to mind three other hapless fishermen dripping rainwater on their floor. The woman noticed that I'd made friends with the St. Bernard (with the help of a spare bratwurst) and said, "He likes to come to town with us, but he's so aggressively friendly he scares the tourists."

By the time we got back on the water the rain had all but stopped, the air had chilled, a patchy fog had settled on the river, and the swarm of spinners had vanished. Jimmy said this "dreaded mist" was a bad sign for the fishing, but as it turned out there were just enough errant spinners and drowned duns on the water to bring the odd trout to the surface and we managed to hook a few. Paul landed the best one: a fat, brightly colored brown about 17 inches long. He was never one to make a fuss over a fish, but he did flash us the impish grin of a kid who's just pulled off something harmlessly naughty.

I first met Paul through his cousin Susan, whom I've lived with for almost thirty years now. In the beginning he struck me as odd and secretive, but I soon realized that he was authentically and unapologetically odd in an endearing way, and instead of being secretive, he was just so steeped in midwestern reticence that he was incapable of either bragging or complaining and so rarely had much to say for himself. We fished together often and I came to enjoy spending time with someone who spoke only when there was actually something to say and was otherwise as silent and self-contained as an owl.

When we met, Paul was a lifelong spin fisherman of the blue-collar school who saw fishing less as a sport and more as just a thing people did for fun and, often enough to mention, for good, free food. When he asked me to show him how to fly-fish, I suspected that he'd see it less as an arcane new method and more as just fishing by other means, and I was right. I checked him out on a fly rod, took him to a mountain creek that's lousy with small trout, and demonstrated how to high-stick a dry fly in pocket water. When his turn came he was into a fish on his third drift.

"Like this?" he asked.

I said, "Yup, just like that."

Bill also claims to have taught Paul to fly-fish. We fight over the credit because he took to it so naturally and got so good so quickly.

What I know about Paul's life before we met amounts to a series of isolated snapshots. He grew up in Charlevoix, Michigan, which is Aspen with yachts to the summer people and hometown to the locals.

He was a Berkeley-educated lighting engineer with a good-paying job, a marriage with two kids—Drew and Heather—an unpleasant divorce (pleasant ones are rare), and friends everywhere, especially in places with good fishing. When he lived in San Francisco he was a neighbor and passing friend of Carlos Santana in the days when the great musician was still schlepping himself to gigs in an old lime-green GMC Gremlin stuffed with guitars and amplifiers. He frequented the psychedelic clubs in the Bay Area at the time and had posters from obscure bands that, unlike Santana, did *not* go down in rock-and-roll history.

Later he became one of the many casualties of the Great Recession. He was laid off from his good job at an age—around sixty—when he was considered too old to hire in spite of his blue-chip education and decades of experience, and sometime later his two modest houses in Michigan were repossessed by the bank. By then Paul had been unemployed for three years in a state with a jobless rate of 16 percent. All he'd say about that time was that he'd fished every day in season, "but not always *all day.*" So he stored what possessions he could stuff into a U-Haul trailer in our garage, sold the rest, and took to doing odd jobs for a living, staying winters in a family house in Charlevoix that was unoccupied for half the year, and spending his summers couch-surfing and fishing with friends.

He was the ideal long-term houseguest: eager to go fishing when that was in the cards and staying out from underfoot when it wasn't. He'd buy his share of the groceries, do his share of the cooking (heavy on midwestern cuisine like sloppy joes and chicken and dumplings), and surreptitiously fix things. One day I'd notice that the window that stuck now slid smoothly and the door that wouldn't latch now clicked shut effortlessly. Whenever he stayed with us the pile of firewood rounds in the yard would continually shrink by small increments, while the stack of split logs on the porch would grow by the same amount. In traditional Michigan fashion, he split wood with a double-bitted feller's ax that he kept sharp enough to shave with.

By the time he got sick he'd had a ten-year run of what anyone would call hard luck, but he seemed to take it all, including his terminal diagnosis, with the same shrugging equanimity and the only time any of it seemed to annoy him was when it cut into his fishing time. But, to be honest, I never really knew what he thought about anything because he mostly kept it to himself, only letting out the occasional hint.

For instance, Paul was always skinny as a rail, even though he was what we used to call in the Midwest a "good eater," and once, before his illness, I watched him polish off an enormous three-course meal followed by a huge wedge of chocolate cake.

I asked, "How can you eat like that and stay so thin?"

He said, "I have to burn a tremendous number of calories to stay this calm."

I came to think of these glancing pronouncements as Michigan haiku: brief, no more than obliquely revealing, and oddly beautiful.

After the Au Sable we drove to Charlevoix, where we stayed in

191

Paul's little house, which is rumored to have once been a garage. For the rest of that week we slept late, lingered over breakfast, killed most of the afternoons, and spent a few slow-paced hours fishing each evening. Paul asked me to do the driving because driving tired him out. We were in my sixteen-year-old pickup, which I'd given to him when I got a new one the year before, and it was comfortably nostalgic to get behind the wheel of it again, although I didn't exactly wish I had it back. The truck wasn't worth much on paper, but I'd kept up the maintenance, changed the oil religiously, and was proud that the old girl still had some life left in her. Paul may have been embarrassed by the gift or just shyly grateful; it was hard to tell. When I handed him the keys and title, he said, "Thanks," but then he was never one for long speeches when a single word would do.

We fished the Boyne, the Pigeon, the North Branch of the Black, the Maple, some of the rivers that boil up out of the Big Swamp and meander north into Lake Michigan. This is Hemingway country, made famous in his Michigan stories published in the 1920s and romantic as hell to me and plenty of others, although the locals are long past being impressed. I never saw it myself, but there's supposed to have once been a bed-and-breakfast here with a handwritten sign in the window that read "Ernest Hemingway Never Slept Here."

The hatches were good and we did well enough most evenings, considering that we didn't hit it all that hard. Paul moved slowly and tired easily. I hung back, wanting him to catch fish; he urged me ahead, wanting *me* to catch fish while he conserved his strength—neither of us quite willing to admit that this wasn't really about fishing.

In August he and his son, Drew, stopped here in Colorado on their way to Drew's house in Hawaii, where, Paul said, he planned to "sit in the sun and think things over until it's time for hospice."

He gave me the address of a friend in New Mexico where he wanted me to send his nearly new boots and waders as soon as he left and then handed me an envelope with ten crisp one-hundred-dollar bills inside.

"What's this?" I asked.

He said, "I sold your truck."

I said, "It was *your* truck and you need this more than I do," and he asked, reasonably enough, "What use do I have for money now?" Then he added, "Don't worry; I sold it to a fisherman."

After Paul took a handful of pain pills and went to bed I offered the money to Drew, but he silently raised his hands and shook his head, a gesture he'd learned from his father. I could see his point. Here was a man with no outstanding debts settling as a matter of pride the few accounts he thought he had. Not something to be trifled with.

Paul had lost weight and color, walked slowly and unsteadily, stopped to rest often, took lots of pills, and just generally seemed to be running on fumes. He said that while he was there he wanted me to take him out to catch what we both knew would be the last few trout of his life. (No pressure, right?)

We got out twice. The first time we went to a stretch of stream where we could fish within sight of the car. Paul fished for an hour and landed three trout before he put down his rod and sat on a log, smiling, but looking done in. He didn't say anything, but when Drew and I suggested that we pack it in he nodded his head. The water where we forded the creek was less than knee-deep and the current was slow, but Drew and I each had to take an arm to get him back across.

The second time we drove to a higher stretch of the same creek. Paul lasted maybe forty minutes, landed two fish on a dry fly, and then asked me to help him back. I put an arm around his shoulders firmly enough to hold him up, but careful not to squeeze what was left of him too hard. The truck was maybe fifty steps away and we had to stop and rest four times. After I unlaced his boots and peeled off his waders I helped him into the passenger seat, where he sat staring blankly out the windshield, breathing hard. I wondered how much the last trout of your life would mean. He may have been wondering the same thing.

Paul died three weeks later. The call came—as those calls always seem to—on the kind of perfect September day when you'd think nothing could possibly go wrong. True to form, there'd been no last words.

Drew and Heather asked if they could come out next summer to go through Paul's stuff in our garage and scatter some of his ashes in the pool where he caught his last trout. I said of course. So when the time comes we'll drive up to the creek with a few of Paul's friends. We'll pick a sunny day in late summer. It'll seem like someone should say something, but none of us will know what. Afterward, maybe we'll do a little fishing.

this is an ideal spot for steelhead to lay up until a change in the light or the temperature or a spate of water signals the fish to move upstream.

Winter steelhead will sometimes roll at the surface, but more often they'll lie deep and sulk and you never know if they're there or not, so the accepted method is to fish big flies deep and slow to match what you imagine to be the mood of the fish. There are plenty of fine points here and some experienced steelheaders have inviolable rules about the size, shape, and color of the fly and whether it should have more tinsel than a Christmas tree or just enough to wink seductively. Some use a heavier tip with an unweighted fly to get deep enough while others prefer a weighted fly with a lighter tip that's easier to cast. And how deep *is* deep enough? Some think you have to stuff the fly right in a steelhead's face, while others believe a fish that swam a thousand miles from midocean to get here will move another two or three feet for your fly. The rest of us just try to check as many boxes as possible under the heading of "common wisdom," eagerly accept the advice of locals, and never shake the suspicion that we're feeling around in the dark for something that might not even be there.

Sometimes swinging flies can seem more ceremonial than practical. After picking what you think is the correct combination of fly and tip to get a swing that feels right, you fish down the run from top to bottom, making two or three evenly spaced steps downstream between casts all the way to the next riffle. You're essentially going through the motions, but the motions include attentiveness to the feel of each swing as the current speed and depth change subtly from one cast to the next. Steelheaders think of themselves as a special breed and it's true that this kind of fishing isn't for everyone. It takes some skill, lots of patience, and most of all hours, days, and weeks of concentration in an era when, as Sam Sacks recently pointed

20.

QUINAULT

Later in the trip I'll wake up harder, but this first morning the sound of my friend Jeff, the camp manager, padding barefoot past the door on his way to start the coffee is all it takes. I swing my legs out of bed, turn off the still-silent alarm clock, and fumble for my clothes without turning on the light so Chris can sleep in if he wants to.

A few minutes later with those first cups in our hands, Jeff and I stand on the back porch watching Quinault Lake and the snow-capped Olympic Range materialize through the rain—everything in shades of predawn gray like a black-and-white photo. Naturally it's raining. This is the rainy season in a temperate rain forest that normally gets two hundred inches a year and it's been the wettest March on record on Washington's Olympic Peninsula. I've yet to spend the week swinging big Intruder flies with a 14-foot rod and 600-grain Skagit head, but as if to remind me that I've spent too many decades standing in cold water in this kind of weather, the usual joints are already beginning to ache from the humid chill: specifically, my left wrist, right shoulder and elbow, and both knees. Other than that, though, I'm still a fine figure of a man.

Off to the northeast the upper Quinault River enters the lake in a wide alluvial fan littered with driftwood snags containing entire uprooted Douglas fir and western red cedar trees that were washed off the banks and downriver to be deposited in piles as the current slowed—testimony that all rivers are works in progress. The Quinault is where we'll be fishing, not because it has all that many steelhead, but because every other river in the region is blown out from the rain.

So far only a few words have passed between us. I'm thinking of other rainy winter steelhead trips to the northwest that I ended with my tail between my legs, either driving the thirty-some hours back to Colorado or calling the airport for an earlier flight home and then fleeing in a rental car before the bridges washed out. Jeff, I'm guessing, is cataloging all the behind-the-scenes chores he has to accomplish in order to keep the guides and fishermen fed, happy, and on the water. If the people who run fishing lodges aren't already chronic worriers when they take the job, they quickly learn to be.

Another fisherman shuffles in and pours coffee and that rouses Jeff from his trance. He bustles into the kitchen to start piles of bacon on a big cast iron griddle and before you know it we're all around the table shoveling in a high-calorie breakfast and bemoaning our collective fates as steelhead fishermen. It's said that these fish are so difficult and time consuming to catch that they eventually

cost devotees jobs, wives, and homes, finally turning them into obsessed loners. It doesn't actually turn out that way very often, but in the company of other steelheaders we pretend that these elusive fish have utterly ruined our lives.

That morning Chris and I launched on the Quinault with young guide named Jeremy, who said he prefers swinging flies w a Spey rod, but spends most of his time with bead and bobber ermen. These are two of the ways fly-fishing for steelhead ca Beads suspended under strike indicators are the more efficie to catch fish, if only because you can cover so much more but there are those of us who prefer to think swinging wit handed rod is classier, more demanding, and just an all-aro tier way to fish.

That's putting it nicely. I'm told that in some circles Sp ermen are seen as stuck-up and pretentious and the met an Old World affectation disguising the fact that we're fishermen. On the other hand, I've heard the bead an characterized as rednecks who believe in Bigfoot, b warming or evolution, and who prefer hatchery ste fish because you can legally kill 'em and eat 'em. I we sometimes view each other uncharitably, but o maintain the pretense of friendliness by waving p to stay out of each other's way, never mind that fashion and territory are at stake.

You're looking for very specific kinds of w in: four to six feet deep, rubble rock bottom, rent on the inside of a faster rip, with the gravelly tail-out at the end of the run. Th more than you might think, actually—b runs that everyone is looking for. There on the Quinault, so you work it hard whe

out in the *Wall Street Journal*, our dependence on cell phones and computers has reduced the average human attention span to eight seconds, or shorter than that of a goldfish. I could say that hooking a fish almost amounts to an interruption of this meditative state, but of course that's crap. Without the slim but real possibility of hooking a steelhead, this would be about as much fun as a colonoscopy.

Given enough time and exposure, it's possible to learn everything you need to know to be an adequate steelheader, although it can't all be taught. For instance, the precise shape the line should describe on the surface and the tug you should feel as the fly swings are impossible to describe. And there's the elusive quality of fishiness: that ineffable quality that allows some enlightened souls to catch fish by doing exactly what you're doing to no avail. It's unbearably spooky, but real, and those who have it can only shrug at your persistent questions, however generous their natures might be.

And in most of the rivers where we now fish for them there's the ability to wrap your mind firmly around the idea that hooking a sea-run fish is so unlikely for any number of reasons that it actually may not happen. The first time I went fishing for anadromous fish was for Atlantic salmon in Scotland. I had a borrowed 14-foot Spey rod with a double taper 10-weight line that I didn't know how to use, but that hardly mattered because there were almost no salmon. This river had been in private hands since the 1740s and had been fished since long before that with hook and line as well as permanent stone fish traps known as cruives, all of which amounted to a sustainable harvest. But by the time I got there the real problems were the myriad global threats to wild Atlantic salmon that are too numerous to list here, and, on a more local level, commercial netting near the mouth of the river that only let in a few straggling survivors—hardly enough to bother fishing for as it turned out. That's an old story and it's the kind of thing they never tell you before a trip, although you'll get hints of it on-site and can learn the details if you ask the right questions.

So before I left for Scotland half a dozen people advised me to get used to the idea that I might not—and in fact probably *wouldn't*—catch a salmon and, sure enough, I didn't. The night before I came home, while sitting in a three-hundred-year-old stone cottage sipping the local scotch they don't export, I said something bravely good-natured about getting skunked. My host winced visibly and said, "Here we say, 'blanked,' lad." It seemed important to get the terminology right. This was the perfect introduction to sea-run fish in the waning years of the twentieth century: all the stodgy old Victorian traditions, including assigned beats and teatime on the river, gillies that acted more like butlers than guides, an actual castle on a nearby hill—and no fish.

But then the first time I went steelheading—with my own Spey rod this time—I caught two. They didn't come easy to a beginner, but they did come, which seemed significant. One was a nice enough hatchery fish with its adipose fin clipped to show its origin and the other was a larger, hotter wild steelhead. I'd heard there was a difference and there was; it roughly corresponded to that between a minivan and a Corvette. I came away with the sense that although many steelhead runs are only shadows of their former selves, these were still fish that could be caught by blue-collar anglers on public water provided they're willing to put in the time and effort.

I've talked to people who say they'd never go after fish that are so difficult to catch—too much risk and expense for too small a return, they say, sounding like investment counselors. I felt that way myself for a long time, but then in the evolving perspective of middle age I somehow acquired a taste for the elaborate flies, the elegantly specialized two-handed rods, and the long dry spells like writer's block between fish. Suddenly it all seemed so irresistibly sophisticated that success brought me back to repeat the occasional stellar performance, while failure brought me back for another try.

That first morning on the Quinault, Chris and I diligently swung the good runs in the rain with our fleece jackets zipped to our chins and the hoods up on our rain slickers. Jeremy had a little butane stove in the boat that he used to make hot soup at lunchtime and later a pot of tea that turned out to be high points of the day.

The next day Chris and I went out with Zack Williams and Trey Combs, who were in camp for a couple of days. I'd met Trey on the Klickitat River a few years earlier, but had known of him long before that through his 1991 book *Steelhead Fly Fishing*. This was my bible when I took up the sport and it's still a rarity among fishing books by virtue of being packed with good information, full of attribution, and containing no authorial preening or ax grinding.

We spread out in the first run right across from the put-in and I buggered my first few casts out of stage fright that Trey Combs could be watching, but then I got interested in reading the run and forgot about it. Once you've worked out the fundamentals, Spey casting is like wing-shooting or public speaking: the less you think about it the better.

Thirty minutes later I'd just about decided that the current was too fast for this to be good holding water when Chris hooked a fish down toward the tail-out. Zack got the net from the boat and we were all on our way down to watch the show when Chris looked up at us with a stricken face and a rod that was still bent, but no longer throbbing. The fish had made one strong run and then ducked into a sunken root ball like a big brown trout. The current was too strong and deep to wade in and try to untangle him, so there was nothing to do except break him off. A lost steelhead is always a tragedy, but any steelhead hooked puts a whole new complexion on things and if your casting has gotten lackadaisical it suddenly becomes crisp and predatory again.

The next day Chris and I took the lodge van back up the Quinault to try some of the runs we'd already fished as well as a few we hadn't but had liked the looks of. It was still raining, but only intermittently now, and small patches of actual blue sky could occasionally be glimpsed through banks of low-lying clouds. The river hadn't dropped any, but it was no longer visibly rising. There was the fresh sense of anticipation you can get with migratory fish, the idea that a pool that was empty or sour a day or two earlier could today be full of newly arrived steelhead, although "full" might not be the right word here.

The night before Jeff and Trey had told us how the Quinault tribe was commercially netting the river downstream on the reservation in an operation Jeff described as "heartbreakingly efficient." I couldn't quite picture the configuration of the nets from his description, but understood they were staggered in such a way that only a fraction of the steelhead could squeeze through to spawn in the headwaters—presumably just enough to maintain the run. There've been discussions with the tribe about letting more fish through, but so far no progress. I wished my friends luck, but wondered how well Native Americans would respond to white guys complaining about the quality of our recreation.

Jeff's wife, Jan, had driven up from Klickitat for a visit and as hors d'oeuvres that night we shared a limit of clams she'd dug out on the coast that day. In this mountainous landscape it was hard to imagine an ocean and a beach just a short drive away, but then the Quinault is a short river as rivers go, just sixty-nine miles from its headwaters at Anderson Glacier in the Olympics to the Pacific.

Jan is an artist and as we sat on the couch talking about friends, she absentmindedly sketched one miniature riverscape after another in a small sketchbook, each one within a frame traced around a credit card. I watched her do four or five of them in a row, each one a really exquisite drawing finished in a matter of a few minutes. When I asked about them she said she imagined an art show in which a thousand of these were hung, face high, in a continuous line that would circle the gallery on an otherwise blank, white wall—minimal, but vast, like a view of the countryside from the window of a moving train.

Later I got into a conversation about steelhead rivers with a guy who'd fished some of those remote locations with famous names, jaw-dropping price tags, and long waiting lists where he'd landed world-class steelhead measuring over 40 inches and hovering in the neighborhood of 20 pounds. The world is smaller and more imperiled than ever, but to hear some tell it you can still find places where enormous silver dream-slabs will happily eat your flies and then proceed to destroy your expensive tackle. Meanwhile, you fish the rivers you can afford.

In subsequent days we floated two other nearby rivers that were said to be dropping and clearing, the Clearwater and the Humptulips, which the guides naturally refer to as "The Hump." They were lovely, densely forested rivers that were a joy to float and fish and they probably held some steelhead, although there was no sign of them. We fished gorgeous glacial-blue runs, swinging so deep we could feel our flies tick the cobbles on the bottom, but no dice.

Back on the Quinault Chris hooked a steelhead on our last day in the last pool we fished. This kind of miraculous save happens just often enough to keep you casting right up until the last possible moment, never mind the hot meal, dry clothes, and warm bed that are waiting when you peel off your waders back at camp. After a week of meticulous swinging he hooked the fish more or less at his feet while carelessly flopping out loose line for his first cast. ("All skill," he'd say later.) I happened to be walking past him on my way to fish the tail-out when he said, "Fish on," in a quizzical tone of voice that almost made it sound like a question. I trotted back to the boat for the net and then stood there holding it at port arms, silently asking no one in particular to please not let me fuck this up.

It turned out to be a fat wild buck weighing about 15 pounds that had been out of salt water long enough to have colored up with wide red stripes down his flanks and pink blushes on its gill covers. After a couple of quick snapshots Chris only had to hold him facing the current for a minute or two before the fish bolted off, splashing water in our faces with his tail.

I've come to love this idea of detaining a fish just briefly enough to admire it and then releasing it as if nothing much had happened. That's not to say that I haven't killed and eaten hatchery steelhead and been happy to do it. (They're genetically inferior to wild fish in every way, but they do spend their lives growing succulent on a diet of high-quality free-range seafood before returning to their home rivers.) On the other hand, I'm now less sanguine than I once was about killing any fish simply because, as Robert Hughes said, "As one gets older one views all death with less indifference."

So I feel that a steelhead stands a better chance with me than it does with seals or gill nets and with proper fish handling our encounter can be just one more close call on its long journey to spawn. Sure, sometimes a non-angler will ask how I can stand to hook, play, and land these increasingly rare fish that I claim to love and respect so much, adding to their already heavy burden of survival. To that I can only say, "It's because life is more complicated than either of us could ever imagine."

21.

DRIFTLESS

Sunday morning in Rushford, Minnesota: The last of yesterday's downpour was still intermittently sprinkling from an overcast but clearing sky and the day was already humid and warm and heading toward hot. It was early and not many people were out yet, but robins were everywhere, drinking from puddles, gorging on drowned worms, and singing their hearts out. After breakfast down the block at Stumpy's Café I piled into the Suburban with Bob White, Mike Dvorak, and Mike's black Lab, Moose, to go looking for a trout stream that was clear enough to fish.

My flight into Minneapolis the day before had been delayed by a 30,000-foot wall of thunderstorms and for a while it looked like we'd have to divert to Chicago, but we finally managed a late, but otherwise uneventful landing on a wet runway. Then on the two-and-a-half-hour drive south into the Minnesota Driftless Area it rained so hard that at times we had trouble seeing the road even with the wipers on high. There were tornado warnings just south of us near the Iowa border, where as much as nine inches of rain had already fallen and Decorah had flooded for the second time in two weeks, but according to the online weather map we were skirting the worst of it, although not by much.

All the streams we crossed were running brown and out of their banks, but Mike, who's guided off and on around here since college and who's unflappable by nature, shrugged it off. "We'll just fish the tributaries," he said. "They'll start to clear by tomorrow." He wasn't guiding now—just fishing with friends—but couldn't resist the guide's impulse to stave off intimations of doom.

The porous limestone geology of the Driftless Area *does* drain quickly, feeding countless cold springs that in turn feed the hundreds of small to medium-size trout streams that had brought us there in the first place. It drains so quickly, in fact, that there's hardly any standing water and therefore no mosquitos—or so the story goes.

The Driftless is a 24,000-square-mile region of the upper Mississippi Valley including parts of Minnesota, Wisconsin, Iowa, and a corner of Illinois. It was missed by the parade of ice age glaciers that plowed the surrounding countryside flat and left behind the layers of clay, sand, gravel, and cobbles known collectively as glacial drift. So unlike the adjacent prairie, the Driftless is all rolling, forested hills, valleys, and ravines and lacks the usual surface layers of drift, hence the name. An easy way to spot the area's boundaries is to look at a road map. On the prairie the roads go straight because the land is flat and there are so few obstacles, but in the wrinkled landscape of the Driftless the roads meander.

We took Main Street out of town past the cemetery and turned up a dirt road that roughly paralleled a medium-size creek. It was off-color where we first saw it—more limestone gray than mud brown—but we were betting it would be clearer upstream, so we drove up the shallow valley past one green, handsome farm after another until we came to Mrs. Anderson's place.

Like most of the streams in the region, this one was entirely on private land, but open to fishing through an extensive state-run easement system. The access points are marked by small turnouts and three-step fence stiles that are either solid or wobbly depending on their age and state of repair. Most fishermen would have had to get in downstream and hike several miles to get to this upper stretch, but Mike has an arrangement with Mrs. Anderson that gives him a shortcut. Once he'd demonstrated that he'd park his vehicle out of everyone's way, close gates behind him, and otherwise act like a gentleman, she was happy to let him on the property to fish. In return she liked a mess of fresh trout for dinner, although she understood that fishing was fishing so she wouldn't hold a slow day against him.

At close range the stream wasn't as muddy as it had looked from the road. The deeper water was still opaque, but there was a fishable 18 inches of visibility along the banks and in the tails of pools. But we only made a few haphazard casts as we worked our way up to the feeder creek Mike had his eye on. It was a first-order tributary fed entirely by springs and with the dense roots of the surrounding woods to hold the soil and keep down the mud.

The creek *was* clear, as Mike had predicted, although where it dumped into the larger stream it looked too small and shallow to be fishable. But then at the first bend there was a pool plenty deep enough to hold trout and it went on like that for the next mile or so until it gradually began to peter out to a trickle. There were stretches of shallow, fishless water separating luxurious pools that looked like they belonged on a larger creek with brown trout that were sometimes bigger than you'd expect from such small water.

We started catching fish right away and I suggested we keep a few of the better ones for Mrs. Anderson, but Mike wanted to wait until we got back down to the larger stream on our way out. He said the fishing would pick up there in the afternoon and we'd be within sight of the farmhouse, so the fish would be fresher. That sounded right and you always want to bow to local knowledge, but in my experience if you intend to keep fish you should keep them while you're catching them because things could change. I actually got a little nervous about this. The fact that she'd understand if there were no trout for her today just made me want to try all that much harder to get Mrs. Anderson her fish.

Of course, Mike was right. By the time we got back down to the larger stream trout were rising sporadically. We got some on dries and droppers, killed and cleaned the four biggest ones, and delivered them to Mrs. Anderson's kitchen door while they were still cool to the touch and before their colors had faded—about as fresh as fish get. She was small, elderly, white-haired, birdlike, a little shy meeting Bob and me as if she were the guest instead of us, and absolutely delighted by the trout. I guessed that she was a widow (if only because women so regularly outlive their men) and that it was her grown children who now kept the lawn mowed and the farm running and freshly painted. Maybe she once fished herself, or maybe her husband and kids once brought her fish, but they're now either gone or can't find the time, so she has to rely on strangers.

All just a guess, of course, and none of my business anyway, but it was still satisfying to bring a few fresh trout to a little old lady. At an age when I've just begun to glimpse little old manhood on my own horizon, it seemed like the kind of outmoded chivalry the two of us would still recognize.

On Monday Bob's poet friend Larry Gavin drove up to fish with us for the day and over breakfast at Stumpy's that morning the conversation was less about which stream to try than about how people like poets, painters, and photographers went about piecing together their uncertain livelihoods. The business end is a separate, but not unrelated aspect of the craft, since the best and possibly only way to get good at anything is to do it for a living. It turned out that, unlike the rest of us, Larry, a schoolteacher by trade, had been smart enough to hold on to his day job.

I rode out with Larry that morning and on the drive to the stream I learned enough about him to conclude that he's what I think of as the other kind of poet. One kind pontificates about his Art and his Process until you're ready to pound your head on the dashboard or hang your head out the window and howl; the other kind is content to let the work speak for itself while he goes fishing. I made a note to order one of his books.

We tried one of the larger streams in the area that, on the second day after the storm, had begun to clear nicely. This region is known for its prolific hatches and we were there in June—a month that dominates the first two pages of the three-page hatch chart— but there were only a few small caddisflies in the air and the occasional boil of a feeding trout. No doubt the storm had put things off for a day or two by raising, cooling, and muddying the water, but now the normal early summer busyness of a healthy trout stream was beginning to kick back in grudgingly, like an old car starting on a cold morning. With nothing more to go on, I tried a size 16 Elk Hair Caddis in case the fish were looking up, with a lightly weighted soft hackle on a dropper in case they weren't—hedging my bet on new water.

We spread out along the stream and went to work. My rig worked well enough that I picked up fish all morning in fits and starts; not a lot, but enough to keep me from wanting to change flies. In one spot I pulled three nice fat brown trout from a seam along a grassy bank in no more than five or six casts, thought I'd hit the motherlode, and then went for twenty minutes without another strike. But for the most part my fish came from here and there at a lazy but steady pace and I enjoyed the sense of being out with intelligent, talkative friends, but alone and silent for the moment.

In the afternoon we drove to another stretch of the same stream and hauled the cooler over to a rough log bench in the shade to have lunch. A few minutes later an old man in baggy hip boots moseyed over and asked if he could sit with us while he rigged up. We said sure and made room for him on the bench, which was still damp from the rain and plastered with dead leaves. He asked if he could sit on the cooler instead. He said, "If I get my trousers dirty my wife will have a fit," in a tone suggesting that of course we men don't care about things like dirty trousers, but you know how women are.

He rigged his rod slowly with his head cocked back to engage the close lenses of his bifocals and his hands fluttering as he threaded the line through the guides. He was still at it when we finished lunch and were ready to stow the cooler he was sitting on and hike downstream, but he seemed so frail and preoccupied that none of us could bring ourselves to ask him to move. So he kept us there for a while as a captive audience, nattering on about this and that—places he'd fished, favorite fly patterns, his wife's preoccupation with laundry. Referring to the two fish dimpling the water over his shoulder, he said that his motto was "never walk away from rising trout." He went on to say that a man he'd once met way out in Montana had given him those as words to live by; someone well known in fly-fishing circles whose name we'd recognize if he could only remember it. "If I had a list of five names I could pick him out," he said, "but I don't."

Eventually he got the rod strung, tied on a small dry fly, lurched to his feet, and started toward the water as Mike deftly snagged the cooler and headed back to the truck with it. Then, after a few steps, he turned abruptly with a finger in the air and said, "Leon Chandler!" You could almost see the lightbulb going on over his head.

A few days later at a fly shop in Lanesboro we learned that this wide bend by the road with its easy wading and unobstructed back cast was known hereabouts as the Old Man's Pool.

Mike took lots of photos on this trip in his usual furtive way. That is, he always had a camera slung over his shoulder and I saw some of the photos later, but I hardly ever actually saw him take one. I'm not sure how he does that. Two of my favorites were some of the crisp black-and-white prints he's best known for. One shows an old bait shop, long since abandoned, but with its sign intact and a load of laundry drying on a line in the background. It's the kind of composition that, like the best acting, leaves you with the sense that you've accidentally glimpsed something small and private. The other was a straightforward portrait of a rough but friendly-looking guy named Arnie that he and Moose met on an early morning walk. Mike has a talent for either catching people in unguarded moments as they go about their business or getting them to look frankly into the lens without the usual posing or camera shyness, a skill he shares with Richard Avedon and Annie Leibovitz.

And Bob did two plein air oil paintings that week; both small studies that were finished works in their own right, but that could also be used as sketches for larger paintings done later in his studio. One looked down a green valley with a bend in the creek in the foreground and a white-painted farmhouse and barn in the distance looking like the kind of place you could go to use the phone if your

211

car broke down and be welcomed with a cup of coffee at the kitchen table. I thought it must be how the farmer himself would have seen the place: lush with water and grass, the good black soil showing where the banks of the stream had sloughed off, and the buildings in the distant background, almost as an afterthought. Bob is famous for his sporting art, but that afternoon, in the heat of the artistic moment, he said he'd like nothing better than to travel around the Midwest painting farms.

The other painting was of a bend in another stream where it leaves the ragged edge of a woodlot and sweeps into an unmown meadow. It was painted on the kind of breezy day when he'd end up with the odd bug stuck in the oil paint—an occupational hazard—and his trees have a liveliness that's reminiscent of Van Gogh's cypresses.

I was fishing that bend the morning Bob carried his easel up the slope above the river and started on that second painting. I didn't have to worry about blundering into the shot the way I would with a photographer. With his painter's omnipotence, Bob would put me in or leave me out as he pleased. There were a few trout dimpling sporadically along the far bank eating the occasional small mayfly and I managed to catch a few chubby brown trout: a good way to start the day.

Mike and Moose had gone downstream earlier and after I felt I'd worn out that bank I thought I'd work my way down there to see how they were doing, but when I came around the bend heading for the next fence stile I found a long, riffly glide that was boiling with mayflies and rising trout. I had a strange moment of indecision. I thought about going back to tell Bob, but I knew he wouldn't stop working. A painting costs him a day of fishing, but he sees that as an opportunity instead of a hardship. Then I thought about going to get Mike, but I didn't know how far downstream he was and for all I

212

knew he was into fish of his own. Then I thought, *never walk away from rising trout.*

The hatch lasted for over an hour and the size 18 parachute I already had on seemed to be the right fly. I didn't hurry; I didn't out-think myself with weird brainstorms about tactics or fly patterns; I didn't flock-shoot, but picked individual fish to cast to. With me success always boils down to a series of characteristic mistakes that for once I didn't make.

When the hatch finally began to peter out, with nothing left but a few splashy rises from small trout, I didn't keep flogging the water hoping for just one more and feeling disappointed; I just reeled in and stood there for a while enjoying the peculiar stillness that befalls a trout stream when a hatch is over. I also didn't count my fish, so probably remember catching more trout than I actually did, which is as good a reason as any not to keep score.

We fished on for the rest of the week, working the tributaries and avoiding the larger rivers, and never really found what you could call clear water. None of the streams were downright muddy, but they were all either beige or milky depending on the local geology, which didn't hurt anything and may have helped. Trout can see better through cloudy water than we can see *into* it and they were hungry and had plenty of visibility to feed, while on our side of things, the off-color water let us fish shorter casts and bigger flies.

Once or twice I caught myself marveling that I'd grown up just a few hours' drive north of here—in the same town where Mike now lives, in fact—and never knew any of this was here. Not that it would have mattered. In those days we fished lakes from boats with silver spoons trailing strips of pickled pork rind, looking for bass and pike. We knew fly-fishing existed, but we weren't sure what it was and a 10-inch brown trout would have seemed like bait, only prettier.

But I did recognize the small, breathlessly quiet rural townships like Arendahl, where there are lots of Arendahls buried in the Arendahl cemetery, most of whom probably went to the Arendahl Lutheran Church just up the road. This is the kind of cradle-to-grave continuity that makes you want to run screaming from the place at fifteen, only to wander back in late middle age wondering if there's something you overlooked the first time around, blinded as you were by angst and hormones.

And I recognized that still, suffocating midwestern heat. It had stayed humid and gotten progressively hotter—well into the 90s by the end of the week. It would have felt good to wade wet, in shorts, but the stinging nettle and caustic wild parsnip that grow shoulder-high along many of these streams kept us baking in hip boots. Back home in the mountain west I'd have at least soaked my hat in weather like this and enjoyed the instant cooling effect of evaporation, but I knew from experience that if I did that in this climate, I'd just end up with a hot, wet hat. I remembered that it was these stifling, humid summers (among other things) that made me want to run screaming, only to eventually settle a thousand miles farther west and five thousand feet higher where the air is thinner and drier, and it's actually cooler in the shade. I can rhapsodize about the beauty of the Rocky Mountains and the western American sensibility that seeps from the landscape like a spring and not be lying, but it didn't hurt that at the time it was the first place I'd ever been where the summers were tolerable.

On my last morning in Rushford I was standing outside my motel room with my first cup of coffee trying to switch gears from a slow-paced week in farm country to the bustle of crowded airports and unforgiving schedules when I finally met one of the guys in the room next door. We'd seen each other coming and going all week, spotted each other as fishermen and waved, but we'd never spoken before. He asked how our fishing had been and I said we'd done well. He said they'd done well, too, both of us being cagey about where we'd gone so as not to give anything away.

"You from around here?" he asked.

I said I lived in Colorado.

"I'm from Michigan myself," he said.

"You've got trout at home," I told him.

"Yeah, so do you," he said, "but there are always other trout somewhere else."

22.

SUCCESS

Thomas McGuane once wrote, "What is most emphatic in angling is made so by the long silences—the unproductive periods." That's how I see it, too. Even on the best day of fishing I ever had, I still did more casting than catching and there've been plenty of days when I did nothing *but* casting. Still, everyone who goes out, including beginners, fully expects to hook and land fish. Likewise, even as you struggle to plunk out a few chords on your first guitar, you can't help imagining the applause of fans, never mind that it's the 1960s, every member of your generation thinks they're a folksinger, and most of them are wrong.

217

So we get ahead of ourselves by nature and envision, among other things, boatloads of fish on the way to our first fly-casting lesson. You can blame some of those unreasonable expectations on a fishing press that tells you exactly where to go and how to catch more and bigger fish once you get there, aided and abetted by a tackle industry that's eager to sell you all the gear you'll need to accomplish that—plus some you won't. But the largest part of it is still just the impatience inherent in the human condition. It can take decades before you begin to feel oppressed by the excessive striving for hotter hot spots and more sophisticated tackle and start groping your way back toward the hometown creek and the single fly box you started with.

I do have the usual collection of big fish snapshots that fishermen accumulate—nothing world class, but all decent or even enviable specimens that seemed worthy of a photo at the time. These four-by-six prints have been thumbtacked one by one to the west wall in my office until they now raggedly frame an Ansel Adams calendar and a watercolor portrait of a de Havilland Beaver floatplane painted by C. D. Clarke. Most are trout, with a few bass, bluegills, char, salmon, steelhead, and a couple of muskies thrown in for variety. The fishy monotony is relieved only by a brace of dead blue grouse posed next to a Bernardelli side-by-side 20 gauge, a plate piled high with wild morel mushrooms, and a UFO photo I faked years ago and sent to a local newspaper as a joke, along with a clipping of the story they printed about the phony sighting.

The few people who have seen this collage must have come away with a false impression of nonstop success: nothing but big fish and lots of them. The most recent photo is of a 47-inch musky from Wisconsin. The oldest—a predigital black-and-white—dates to the 1970s and shows me as a much younger man holding a 25-inch rainbow/cutthroat hybrid from a lake in Montana. (At the time it was the largest trout I'd ever caught and it's still right up there.) But given the time span covered, all those photos average out to only slightly more than one exceptional fish per year. And I've done quite a bit of fishing.

As hard as I've tried, I can't quite remember my first trout on a fly. Wishful thinking wants to make it a brook trout, but it's more likely to have been a brown or even a stocked rainbow. I want to say it took an Adams, but it could just as easily have been an Elk Hair Caddis. I do know it was a dry fly, though. Back then nymphing was still frowned upon by the intelligentsia as no better than bait fishing, so I'd become an insufferable dry fly purist before I'd even hooked a fish—at least on paper.

But I do remember the long drought that preceded that first fly-caught trout as the longest of many subsequent long silences, and I remember that it stretched on until I finally developed the habit of secretly carrying bait hooks and sinkers for days when trout were on the menu. Years later, when fishing subsurface with a fly rod became politically correct, the memory of drifting a worm behind a split shot gave me a real leg up as a nymph fisherman.

That first long dead spell—and the other, mercifully shorter ones that followed—amounted to an apprenticeship that, if nothing else, gave me common cause with other anglers and fine-tuned my bullshit detector. Also, nothing teaches you how to effectively study the water for missed clues like being reduced to tucking your rod under your arm and watching because you've run out of options. Still, we measure ourselves by our successes if only because our many failures—unless they're downright Shakespearan—don't make for much of a story. And fishermen do love their stories.

One of the best beaver ponds I ever fished was in the mountains of northern Colorado, half a mile and several hundred feet below a cirque lake that had been stocked years before with grayling and golden trout. Beavers had dammed the outlet stream at the bottom of a meadow, backing up a lake-size pond that was populated by grayling up to 15- or 16-inches long and a few cutthroats of about the same size, plus one trout I couldn't identify.

I assumed it was a cutthroat because it had the characteristic red slashes on its jaw, but everything else seemed wrong. Its flanks were a coppery yellow color, it had white-bordered anal and dorsal fins like a brook trout, and bruise-colored parr marks as well as the usual uneven sprinkling of black spots. With a friend's help I got a few pretty clear color photos of it that I sent to Robert Behnke, the famous fisheries biologist and trout guru at the University of Colorado. He wrote back that without a necropsy he couldn't give me a firm identification, but that based on the fish's markings and where it was caught, his best guess was that it was a golden/cutthroat hybrid. Not something you see every day.

I had to go back to the photo to remind myself of the fish, but I can still close my eyes and picture that beautiful spot. The biggest beaver pond I've ever seen in the Rocky Mountains was tucked into a high bench surrounded by spruce forest beneath steep peaks turning amber in the late afternoon September sunlight, everything fantastically foreshortened by the thin, dry air that was so clear it shrank a mile down to a hundred yards. The trout and grayling were as big and fat as they'd get that summer and even after we'd caught and released all the fish we could possibly want, we had trouble tearing ourselves away. But finally we hiked down to the vehicle so we could four-wheel out in what was left of the daylight. This wasn't the worst Jeep road I'd ever driven, but it was the kind where headlights would be useless because most of the time the beams would be lurching through the treetops, leaving the road ahead in darkness.

As fisheries, beaver ponds have the same tragically short life spans as beloved pets and that was one of the handful of great ones I've fished, but there are countless others I scouted before and since that were either too new to have grown big fish yet, or were silted in, blown out, gone stagnant and sour, or were otherwise past their brief prime. As I said, all those blank days don't make for much of a story in their own right, but taken together they amount to the interminable setup for a joke that turns out to be worth the wait when the punch line finally arrives.

Fishing has never lent itself to the kind of satisfaction on demand that technology has trained us to expect for the simple reason that fish don't want to be caught and go to great lengths to avoid it. That's why it doesn't make sense to take up fly-fishing for the bragging rights alone; it's better to see it as an acquired taste that reintroduces the chaos of uncertainty back into our well-regulated lives. Fishermen who care too much about the size and numbers of fish they catch are insufferable on good days and as harried as overworked executives on slow ones. On the other hand, it's possible to be a happy angler who doesn't catch many fish; it's just that no one will ever say you're good at it.

Still, some get stuck on the idea of racking up a score and spend their fishing time pursuing bonanzas. They might chase major hatches around the country the way others follow favorite rock bands, or congregate in Alaskan fish camps during silver salmon runs where, if their timing is right, they can land big fish until they're no longer able to lift their arms. Their dispatches home contain reports of major tonnage.

Others go for size. In the Northwest they'll prefer Chinook salmon over steelhead, in salt water they'll look for tarpon in the 100-pound range, or maybe they'll spend weeks flogging Pyramid Lake in Nevada hoping for a 20-pound Lahontan cutthroat. Once these trophies would have been mounted by a taxidermist and hung on a wall where their colors would gradually fade, their jaws would come unhinged, and their fins would fray; now they're more likely to be memorialized as digital images on fishermen's cell phones, where they'll always be fresh and bright and just a swipe away.

A subspecies of the big fish guy is the local loner who haunts ordinary rivers, peering into deep holes and undercut banks looking for the fat, hook-jawed old brown trout that turn up from time to time even in water that's not known for big fish. These bruisers are rarely if ever seen because they shun daylight, fatten up secretly after dark on fish and rodents, and because most fishermen don't believe they're even there and so don't hunt for them.

I heard about a guy like that when I fished the trout country in southeast Minnesota recently. He was said to locate, mark, stalk, and eventually catch enormous trout in water where most locals were happy with a 15-incher. The proof was in the photos he'd occasionally post on social media of him cradling trout 30 inches long or better and weighing many pounds while wearing the expression of someone who'd just committed the perfect crime. He never revealed his fly patterns or the locations where those fish were caught and it was said that he fished alone in order to maintain secrecy, although he must have had an accomplice because someone had to take the pictures. Some people who knew him said he was sort of an odd duck.

And there are the problem solvers who gravitate to the most difficult fish, like spoiled spring creek trout that feed on blanket hatches of insects in glass-clear water and, with the help of countless skilled fishermen every season, have developed a talent for smelling the rat in even the most perfectly tied and flawlessly presented fly patterns. You'll see these guys standing motionless on the bank studying first the rise forms on the water and then the contents of their overstocked fly boxes, pondering questions that, judging by their expressions, border on the metaphysical. These are the people Charlie Waterman was referring to when he described fly-fishing as "a small pool of trout surrounded by a great wall of speculation."

Still others go the full distance to steelhead and salmon, anadromous fish that come and go seasonally but unpredictably and are genetically programmed not to feed when they return to fresh water to spawn so they don't eat up their own descendants. Trying to work out when and why they'll sometimes eat a fly anyway is like describing the sound of one hand clapping and these fish have been subjected to generations' worth of far-fetched theories and outlandish fly patterns. It's true that all successful strategies are based on a plausible supposition, but in my experience gamblers and fishermen with a "system" exhibit unshakable confidence, but don't actually do any better than the rest of us.

And in northern Wisconsin, where I've been fly-fishing for muskies for the last few years, the guides rightly believe that these fish have everything for connoisseurs of size and difficulty. Not only are they the fish of a thousand casts, but for those who favor foot-long flies lobbed on thunder-stick rods, a day of musky fishing is a physical workout akin to eight hours of splitting wood. And if you do finally catch one it can be four feet long and there's the added drama of trying not to get bit.

The last time I went musky fishing I ended up in a jet sled on the Flambeau River with Luke, the guide who, on previous trips, had gotten me into my biggest fish. Luke and I get along well, but there's an almost half-century difference in our ages, so while I'm sort of old school (comically so, as he sees it) Luke and his boat both bristle with the latest available technology.

A new addition this year was a pole bolted to the console holding a pair of GoPros that were set to run continually and record an entire day's fishing. Luke explained that to operate a successful guide service now you have to be all over the Internet with constantly updated, professional-quality material, and since I'd heard this from others I supposed it was true. Still, this setup made me uncomfortable at first, although I quickly got involved in the fishing and forgot all about it, which may be the whole point. I guess it just comes down to that age difference. People of my generation still lug around an antique presumption of privacy, while those in their twenties seem okay with being under constant surveillance and probably assume that at this stage of human evolution we're all just bit players in someone else's movie.

It was the last day of a slow trip—well past the thousand-cast mark without a take or even a follow—and we'd exhausted the speculation about why we weren't seeing any fish. It had rained hard recently, cooling the water and raising the river to the point that lily pads could be seen two feet below the surface, but after the heat of summer that should have been beneficial. And the water had darkened from its usual clear but tannin-stained tea color to a shade closer to root beer, changing the color of my huge white streamer from pink to orange to red as it sank, but that shouldn't have made any difference, either.

Late in the afternoon the other fisherman in the boat, Steve, asked if we'd drop him off at the boat ramp where he'd stashed his car that morning so he could get an early start on his long drive home. He didn't seem especially discouraged after several days of unproductive casting, but he did seem like a man who'd seen the writing on the wall. So for the last hour or so of that last day, Luke and I were both fishing. Strictly speaking, the guide doesn't fish when there's a client in the boat, but if anyone asked, we could say the day was officially over and we were off the clock, or that we just really wanted to put a fish in the boat before we called it quits, or that we'd begun to move beyond the whole guide/client arrangement and were now just fishing together as friends, all of which would have been true enough.

When Luke hooked a fish it was a tremendous surprise, partly because there'd been so little action on this trip and partly because hooking a musky is such a rare event that it's *always* a surprise. Things happen quickly when one of these fish is hooked, so however experienced you are, there's always yelling, and splashing, and fumbling with the big landing net, and shouted instructions that sometimes no longer apply to the current situation even before they're out of your mouth.

I got the fish in the net on the second try (feeling that queasy mix of elation and jealousy that descends when someone else catches a nice one) and from there on out it all went smoothly. Luke measured the fish; it was a respectable musky at 45 inches. I took a couple of photos with his cell phone, the usual hero shots with Luke smiling proudly and the musky delivering the blackly murderous stare of a captured predator. And then, within seconds, the fish was back in the water recovering, and then it was gone under its own steam—one of the finest moments in fishing.

When Luke got around to checking the two GoPros, he found that the pole had somehow gotten turned 90 degrees, so that the entire day's worth of footage consisted of nothing but the passing riverbank. (I swear I had nothing to do with that, although I wasn't sorry to hear the news.) I thought of what, for my young friend, would have been an expired cultural reference: Andy Warhol's strange 1964 silent film *Empire*, which consisted of an eight-hour and five-minute sustained static shot of the Empire State Building during which nothing happens except the passage of time. I couldn't help imagining an avant-garde fishing film consisting of an uneventful eight hours and five minutes of passing riverbank. You could call it "A Fisherman's Life."

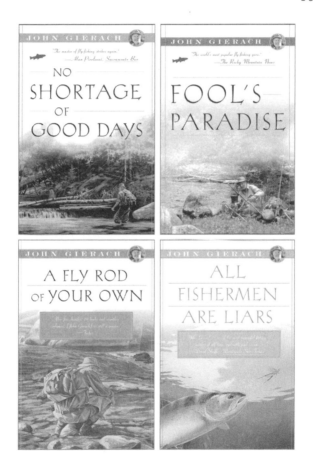